FOOTBALL *days*

REFEREE
F.I.F.A.

FOOTBALL
days

Classic Football Photographs by Peter Robinson

Foreword by Michael Palin

Text by Will Hoon

MITCHELL BEAZLEY

I dedicate this book to the memory of my father, Christopher Robinson, and "The Bishops" – Bishop Auckland FC

FOOTBALL DAYS
Photography Peter Robinson
Design Doug Cheeseman

First published in Great Britain in 2003 by Mitchell Beazley
An imprint of Octopus Publishing Group Ltd., 2–4 Heron Quays, Docklands, London E14 4JP
Reprinted twice 2003
First published in paperback 2005

Commissioning Editor Mark Fletcher
Executive Editor Kate John
Executive Art Editor Christine Keilty
Editor Henry Russell
Production Gary Hayes
Proofreaders Mike Evans, Richard Guy
Indexer Sandra Shotter

A CIP record for this book is available from the British Library

ISBN 1 84533 161 3

Produced by Toppan Printing Co., (HK) Ltd.
Printed and bound in China

page 2
Billy Bremner and Ron Harris
Leeds United v Chelsea
FA Cup Final 1970

contents page
AC Milan v Juventus
European Cup Final 2003
Manchester, England
28 May 2003

CONTENTS

FOREWORD
By Michael Palin

Football, for all its shortcomings, gross inequities and embarrassing inadequacies, is embedded in the national and international psyche like no other sport.

Since I was old enough to know the difference between Sheffield United and Sheffield Wednesday (red and white stripes instead of blue and white stripes), my life has been measured out in Saturday afternoons, (or more recently, in Sunday lunchtimes and Wednesday evenings as well). Not knowing my team's results, in however trivial an encounter, is a bit like losing the feeling in one of my legs.

Any suffering has been mitigated by the wonders of modern communications. I've savoured news of a Blades win over Hartlepool whilst bobbing across the Persian Gulf on a dhow, and agonized through an England–Spain penalty shoot out whilst white-water rafting on the upper Amazon.

Why should it matter so much? Why has so much of my life seemed less important than the football results? Well, the short answer lies in the book you have before you. What Peter Robinson has caught so well is that the primary appeal of football is emotional. It allows us, indeed encourages us, to expose feelings that we have been taught to keep quiet about. As we watch a football game we publicly express extremes of elation and depression which a psychiatrist might take months to prise out of us.

This curious quality which elevates football from being simply a game in which a round object is kicked about by 22 people to something which allows us to rise above the everyday, to become giants through our heroes, is what this book is all about. And it's all done with images. Images as eloquent as any words.

Look at the faces of the crowd in Robinson's photograph (*opposite*) of Bobby Charlton as he prepares to take a corner kick and you could be looking at the crowd in a Renaissance painting, watching water being turned into wine or dead men brought back to life. There is the same rich collection of faces and expressions, the same foreshortened perspective, the same intensity of expectation. There's no doubt about it, there are elements of a religious experience here; the focussing of collective psychic energy around one man whose kick might, at least for an hour or two, change lives.

It's not just the subjects that make Robinson's work so memorable. It's how he presents them. He pushes up strong colours and emphasises hard contrasts of light and shade, which together with clever cropping, make for vivid, dramatic images; George Best apparently alone against a background of green turf, masked Roma supporters shrouded in a sulphurous mist that looks suspiciously like hell-fire.

For all but the luckiest football supporters the moments of triumph are few and far between, and the general lot of football fans is, at the very best, stoic tolerance. Robinson captures the unity of grief in what is perhaps my favourite photograph of the collection, in which a group of disconsolate Leicester supporters trail home along Filbert Street after relegation from the Premiership. Their heads are down but their balloons remain defiantly perky. It is a beautifully observed small moment. A playwright could spend several scenes setting up such a situation, telling us who these people are and why they're thinking what they're thinking. Robinson has it in one.

He is good, too, at the landscape of football, the relation of the game to its surroundings. Football has always been, though it is perhaps less so now, a celebration of community, and the appeal of the game cannot be fully understood without understanding who is watching and where they've come from. Once again his pictures speak volumes. The church behind the barbed wire at Goodison Park. The bleak houses on the Huddersfield skyline as Frank Worthington practices his ball skills, the arched entrance to Charlton Athletic's ground springing out of a terraced street in the East End, a bowls match beside the ground at Cheltenham, a cabbage patch upstaging Yokohama's mighty World Cup stadium.

Robinson understands the visceral appeal of the game. He appreciates the organic relationship of player to the turf, with picture after picture reminding us of the pitch as a living thing. I particularly like the reminders of those days when football and mud were inseparable, largely because my own experience as a centre-half was being sent out on pitches from which almost every blade of grass had been scoured and one sliding tackle could leave a trench deep enough to take a small tree.

There are moments of tragedy; few more telling than Robinson's dark image of England's last game at Wembley, with rain and cushions pouring down in disgust. He doesn't shirk the violence which stalks the game, but balances it with nice touches of humour; the solemn Russian squad who've soiled themselves in a pre-photo knock about, the shirt with a "2" inked in beside the 1, a line of training players prancing round the perimeter of their ground which bears the stern warning: "Please Keep Off The Pitch".

If there is such a thing, Peter Robinson is a romantic realist. He understands the sentiment in which the game is mired, without ever being sentimental. He celebrates the glamour whilst acknowledging the greed and corruption that follows in its wake.

For all the attempts to define it, codify it, and turn it into an industry, football remains a sport, and in sport, the heart ultimately rules the head.

Peter Robinson understands the heart and soul of the game. His eye is generous, caustic, thoughtful and celebratory and although I feel sure that he is too modest a man to assume anything conclusive, these photographs offer as subtle and incisive an insight into the appeal of football as you could hope to find.

Football Days brings the game to life.

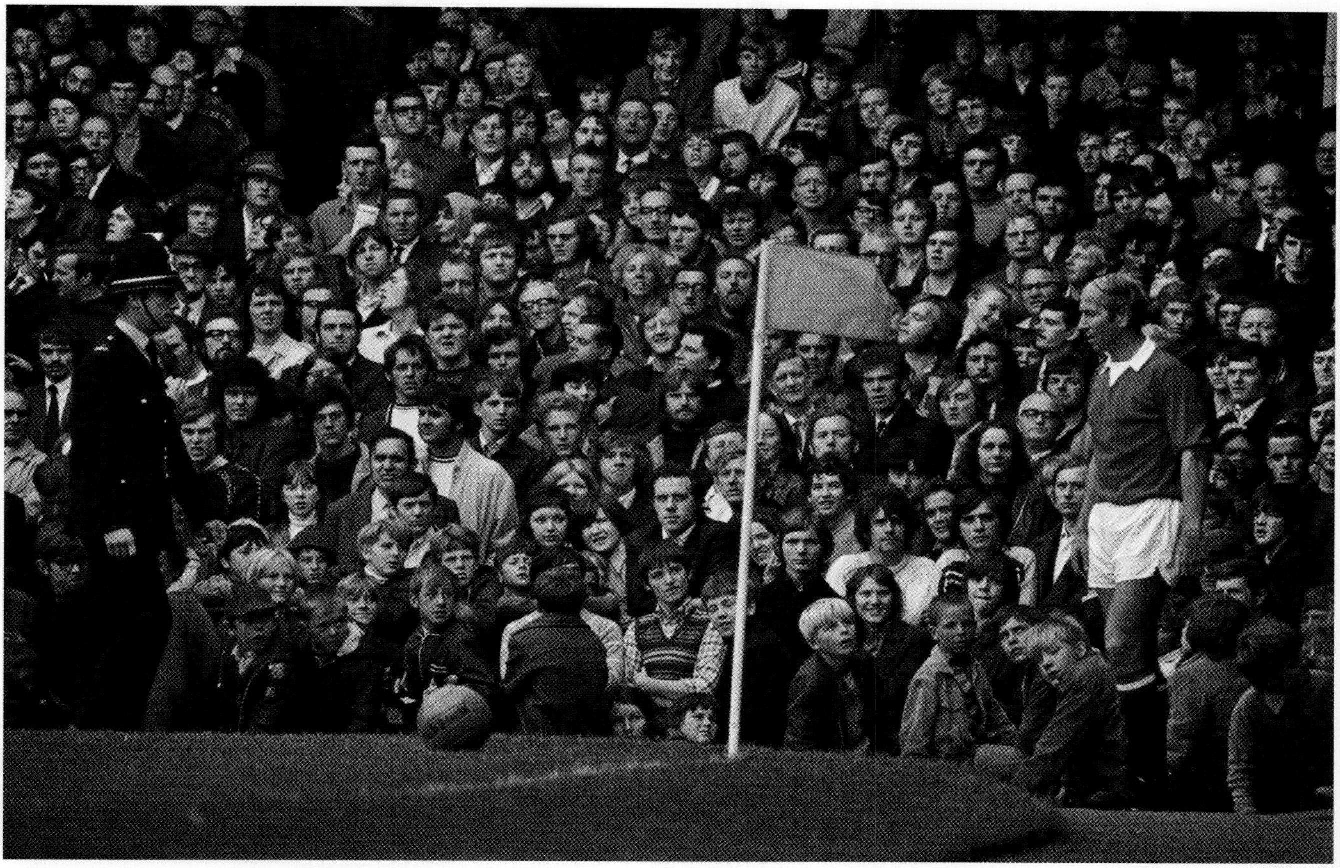

Bobby Charlton
Wolverhampton Wanderers v
Manchester United
c 1970

INTRODUCTION

Peter Robinson has been a photojournalist since 1967. A graduate of The Royal College of Art, his work as a sports and documentary photographer has always been rooted in his love of cinema. A specialist in football, he was until 1994 the official FIFA photographer. In the mid- to late '70s he worked for *Sports Illustrated* in New York and *Onze*, the influential football magazine in Paris. In the '80s Eastman Kodak appointed him their special photographer and he shot the Winter and Summer Olympics and the Asian Games amongst other events. In 1985 he was also asked by Kodak to curate an exhibition in Beijing of his own work – believed to be the first by any foreign photographer in China. He has also been photographer to the Camel Trophy/Land Rover 1,000 mile off-road event in Madagascar, and has curated and staged photography exhibitions in Paris, London and Tokyo.

Would you call yourself a sports photographer?
Probably not, although maybe I should as I have always had to earn a living, and a large proportion of my working life as a photographer has been spent at sports events around the world working for newspapers and magazines.

However, I started off as a documentary photographer, trying to tell stories with photos, but always really wanting to be a film-maker.

My first attempt at sports photography, though, was a project I gave myself at art school. Manchester United had won the League Championship in 1965 and George Best was reputed to be receiving over 1,000 letters a week from fans. I was just in my first year at Leicester School of Art and Design, and he seemed the ideal subject for a budding celebrity photojournalist and possibly easier to get to than the Fab Four. My folks had bought me a camera, I don't remember what make, but it wasn't the top of the range – perhaps Russian – and I borrowed a telephoto lens from a chemist's shop because chemists also sold cameras and film in those days.

The equipment was a bit of a lash-up really, nothing like what I use today, but it worked. When the photo pass arrived in the post I couldn't believe my luck: the club were marvellous and let in this impoverished student without asking too many searching questions.

I was broke and hitched to Manchester. Because film was expensive I rationed myself to two rolls, so it was to be one roll for both halves and the other roll for hopefully hanging around outside the stadium waiting for Best to appear and capturing some close-up portraits.

I really responded to the opportunity of being one of the few on the field and not one of the masses in the stands: it was pure elitism. I was in my element, but unfortunately I got carried away on the game and used both rolls, so the portraits had to wait another three years. I have still got two of the pictures I did on that day. Best (*right*) is looking very thin and boyish with a mass of long wavy hair, quite unlike 99 per cent of footballers who all had short hair, and that was possibly why he was called the fifth Beatle. He looks vulnerable and beautiful too, I think I can say that, in an as yet unspoiled way. Of the pictures I made, most were of him standing, not moving: I don't think I could have mastered the action technique in a few hours. He was some distance away so I used the telephoto I borrowed from the shop. I made a three-quarter length profile of him that showed how thin he was and how the shorts and the shirts fitted him – he is just standing with his hands on his hips. Considering when I photographed him, his position in the frame is quite interesting because even though he is the star I haven't put him in the middle of the frame, I've pushed him to one side. It was instinctive; it just seemed the correct composition. I suppose I am hinting at a future as yet uncertain.

What influence did your family have on your choice of photography as a career?
Neither of my parents had any great interest in photography. My father was a police officer and that was also the career he had mapped out for me. My mother, however, had some success as a swimmer, representing Great Britain at the Berlin 1936 Olympics, and my proudest possessions are her medals.

Because of my interest in film and success with the school's movie camera, and despite my father's expectations for me, I enrolled at Leicester Art School on a three-year photography diploma course. From the first day it was clear to me that I had hit on what it was I wanted to do, maybe not for ever because that seemed too far off, but at least for the next few years. The school had excellent facilities, enthusiastic staff; it was difficult not to feel inspired.

As far as art school was concerned, Best was my first and only attempt at sports photography because the celebrity aspect of football was what had interested me, and apart from Best there was not a lot else to photograph in football in my opinion.

After my father recovered from his disappointment and realized I wasn't going to be the Chief Constable of Leicestershire he was very supportive, as was my mother, and when I started working at it I was never short for equipment – I suspect now that they went into debt to keep me shooting.

My father came to Leicester from Durham in the early '40s looking for work. He was passionate about football and went to Leicester City regularly but never lost his attachment for the North-East and regularly regaled me with stories about his team – Bishop Auckland – that had played in front of 100,000 people at Wembley and won the Amateur Cup 10 times.

What was your first assignment?
There was a football magazine that was being printed and produced from Leicester and I was

George Best
1965

between colleges and of course unemployed, so I got a cash-in-hand job delivering the magazines from the printer to out-of-the-way places – I must have been about 20 or so then. Anyway, the publisher found out that I had a camera and asked me to take some match photos at my next destination.

So I left late on the Friday, slept overnight in a ropy old Bedford van and got the highly desirable opportunity to photograph Torquay United Football club on the Saturday. It was Torquay versus somebody (as usual I can't remember those important details) and that was the first game I actually photographed professionally. Not really for money because I was paid to deliver magazines.

I thought it was all amazing – sleeping in a lay-by in Somerset, in a van with no heater, in November. I got paid on distance so as you can probably guess Torquay United came to figure large in my portfolio.

Was football part of your life at school?
Unfortunately I never played football, only rugby. It just wasn't that sort of school. But football was in the blood – I started supporting Leicester City early on, as I was taken to Highbury by my father to see the FA Cup Semi-Final, Leicester against Portsmouth, in 1949. It was part of his conditioning process – I was only five years old. I became an avid supporter of Leicester City for a few years in my teens, and for a time Saturday at Filbert Street (*see p. 59*) couldn't ever come quick enough. But other interests took over and it wasn't until I went to photograph Best that I understood what a part football played in people's lives and how as a photographer I might record that.

So when I started to photograph football I followed that through – I just picked up on anything that was visually interesting or had good story possibilities, particularly with the fans. If a goalkeeper looked odd or one of the goalposts was a bit tilted or I was able to photograph from an off-limits position, it all went into my visual notebook for that particular game. I couldn't see the point in being there unless I reacted to what was going on in the whole of the ground.

The top sports magazines such as *Sports Illustrated* were in the USA, and I had seen enough pictures by their photographers to know that celebratory imagery of sports events, whilst technically flawless, didn't strike me as that interesting, and although eventually I did become one of their photographers, in 1966 I had no desire to become a regular sports photographer. My photographic references then were such as Elliott Erwitt, Walker Evans, William Klein, and Robert Frank – all Americans except for the Swiss, Robert Frank.

Erwitt liked quirky slices of life, odd juxtapositions of things; Evans was looking at vernacular subject matter, Klein the painter turned street photographer, and Frank without doubt the most important photographer in the last 60 years. I looked for their preferred subjects in a football context, and at the start tried to ape their style. I just hope I added enough of myself to the mix.

How has football photography changed during your career?
Because of the technical difficulty in recording moving subjects in the early days photographers were not attracted to sport. Although group photographs of teams were possible, eventually there were of course advances in lenses and emulsions, and action photography became the norm, but in the history of photography football imagery is a notable omission. By 1960 it was about 40 years since press photographers had first recorded football matches on a regular basis, yet even by the late '60s where one photographed from and what one photographed and the way football was represented hadn't really changed in 40 years – and actually I don't think England had changed very much at all socially, either. The social and class structure was entrenched, and nothing changed really until the masses had got some spare money in their pockets around the start of that decade.

If one looks at the photography around that time in the sports pages of, for instance, the *Daily Mirror*, it's quite clear that, apart from changes in fashion, the style of newspaper sports photography is no different to the way it had been for the last 40 years.

So although I wasn't around in the late 1930s I was still getting the flavour of those times because I worked with and knew photographers who had also worked during that period with plate cameras – large-format cameras that used sheet film instead of film on a roll or in a cassette. Take a picture, pull out the slide, turn it over and use the other side. No third image: you couldn't wind on quickly and take another shot. Your instinct for the right moment had to be spot on, your timing had to be very, very good.

By 1970 Nikon and other Japanese manufacturers had developed the motor-driven 35mm camera and we had access to high-quality German telephoto lenses so it was possible to shoot from any place in the stadium and still get a good picture. Some sports photographers saw this as a creative opportunity and exploited the equipment to its full potential, but it was still only a recording of the event, albeit from a different angle.

Today photographers can send pictures back down the mobile phone line to the office or newspaper, no need for shipping film or complicated mobile darkrooms. They shoot and then they look at the display on the back of the digital camera or on the laptop computer. If it excites them, they transmit it via the Internet. If it doesn't, they delete it.

So it's shoot, view, decide, transmit or delete – almost as quick as I say it. The technology is awesome, but rest assured next year even this will be old technology.

Rivaldo and Ronaldo
2002 World Cup Final

Tell me about your equipment.
It's a mix of cameras and lenses – Leica, Canon, Nikon and Hasselblad, some digital. Usually I take three cameras with me. I occasionally use a long lens; the fact is I have to make a living, and to make a living photographing football for magazines and newspapers you need a certain sort of equipment. So the telephoto lens and digital get used more often than not.

What are you looking for – is it a beautiful picture?
When I am working I never think about beauty, I think only about how I can communicate the essence of the image that's presented to me. After I have made the photograph, that's the time to consider whether it's beautiful or not. Generally though, because I'm a documentary photographer and not a painter, it's a battle trying to deal with the limitations of the medium and what has defined artistically acceptable press photography for a very long time. The aesthetics of contemporary sports photography are hindered in my view by an over-emphasis on appearance, focus, mood and "the decisive moment".

The notion of what sports photography might mean can't be addressed in a newspaper because there is no room on the sports pages for ambiguity or abstraction. I'm not putting sports photographers down because I know from my own experience how fine the difference is between having "the picture" and not having it, and also I'm aware of the demands placed on the photographer by himself sometimes, but usually by the editor looking for the one picture that tells the whole story.

But the need to have "the moment" is what I see as press photography's weak spot, and sports photography, even though it was practised to such great effect by *Sports Illustrated* stars like Neil Leifer, hasn't in my view moved on very far from where it started over 70 years ago.

That photo of Ronaldo and the fan in the Yokohama Final in 2002 *(facing page and p. 141)*: why was this selected?
It was the end of the game and I was about one metre away from Ronaldo and Rivaldo as they ran round the field together with the World Cup in shot. There was also this Brazilian fan, in glasses with lenses that gave him this mad staring look: he had his arms round Ronaldo's waist and just wouldn't let go, everywhere Ronaldo went he dragged this fellow along.

Part of the fan's face was pushed into Ronaldo's back and he was looking at me as I made the picture; for him it didn't matter whether it was me or who it was taking the photo, whether he would ever get a copy or that he would ever see it published. The knowledge that somebody had recorded the moment was sufficient for him and I connected with his need totally. In my view, he improves what is no more than a regular football celebration.

Many of the pictures in this book are rather enigmatic. Were they chosen for that reason?
I suppose I am asking the viewer to not read the pictures one by one, but to take the book as a whole. Many of these pictures are puzzling or paradoxical. This frankly is my intention. I'm asking the reader to work a bit and speculate what might be going on overall.

Did you think the World Cup in 2002 would be your last?
Hopefully not, because if I do Germany [2006] it will be my 10th World Cup. Although when I arrived in Seoul (*pp. 94–95*) in May 2002, knowing I was reaching 60 and it was going to be bloody hard work – constant travelling, irregular hours and chaotic organization – I was wishing then that France had been the last. But at the end of the Final in Yokohama, Brazil had done their celebrating and all was quiet in the stadium, I felt marvellous but disappointed that it was all over as I packed my equipment away – in fact not too dissimilar to after the game at Old Trafford almost 40 years ago. Maybe, though, in 2006 I will be making a film of the event – anyway that's my plan.

You and football – an odd couple. You are not really a fan yet you stick with it – why?
I'm a huge fan of the game generally, just not one team in particular. It suited me to see it that way. Because football is so structured – the games are all to a calendar – I was able to fit it all in easily with my other work. If I had to shoot in Germany midweek I could stay on and cover football in possibly four other countries before returning to England a week later.

I used the same logic in South America or Asia, although the distances travelled were far greater. There was no specific reason I continued doing this for so long, I never intended to make it my life's work... but it seemed hard to stop once I had gotten started.

It seems then there is something about you that is right for football...
I am one of the very few people that feels the need to interpret football in the way that you see in this book. I suppose I am always searching like the hunter, reading the signs on the ground: I smell things out. I am interested in everything that happens at a football match, not just the big moment when the ball goes in the net. I am as excited by the sideshows as the main event, but mostly by people removed from the crowd. I never carry a dossier in my head of the strengths and weaknesses of the teams, I just follow the signs and make it up as I go along. One day I may choose to photograph this way, the next day it's completely different. Sometimes I simply report the game as a newspaper photographer might.

An example of that would be the 1999 European Cup Final between Bayern Munich and Manchester United (*below*). On that

Manchester United
European Cup Final 1999, Barcelona

Heysel Stadium
29 May 1985

particular day I didn't shoot any of those sideshow pictures I mention. I had problems getting into the Nou Camp in Barcelona, and when I finally did, I sensed this was not the game to go hunting and I ought to take as few pictures as possible, and then only with wide-angle lenses. Of course totally against the grain for me I finished up with all the important goal pictures and the line-up of Manchester with the trophy – not what I normally expect.

What was your role at the Football League and how did this come about?

Around 1967 a sports journalist named Harry Brown convinced the Football League that they should publish a mini-magazine called *Football League Review* and insert it into club magazines. I guess the idea was to hit all 92 clubs, which would have given the magazine a very large circulation, but many clubs objected to what they saw as a dictatorial attitude by the Football League. Nevertheless many did take it, including some of the big clubs such as Arsenal. My job was to drive around the country and dig up football stories and anything that had good visual possibilities.

I was given total freedom to shoot anywhere and any way I wanted, and because I hadn't come from a newspaper sports background my references were football versions of what I stole from the pages of style magazines like *Nova* or *Town*, or the German magazine *Twen*, or maybe even the covers of album sleeves from Blue Note Records.

I photographed team groups in every crazy formation I could imagine and, assuming the club did not object, it all found its way into print. Coincidentally Arsenal (*below and pp. 72–73*) came in for this treatment quite often. Not that any of this was avant-garde – it wasn't, but at least the FL published the work, and though the magazine was small and the paper was poor it became my own personal portfolio for every good or half-baked idea I ever had.

And FIFA?

A lot different.

Because I knew the FA people, it was inevitable that when FIFA decided they needed a photographer for the World Cup in 1970 in Mexico I would be appointed to do it. However, I found out when I arrived that all they really wanted from me was a record of official meetings and suchlike. So there was little photography done by me on the games in those early days, although that changed later.

I have to say that FIFA's requirements were always very clear: they needed straightforward, unambiguous photography for their reports and documentation. So there was not much opportunity for off-the-wall photography. Our association lasted for 24 years and during that time I was witness to the most important period in international football.

What does this collection constitute?

Because it's work culled from such a long period [38 years], as a collection it's impossible to say this a concise body of work in a fixed style. The intention of each photograph is quite different. Sometimes it's purely a document – in other words cold informative and objective – at other times a puzzle. But generally it's a form of intensive looking that speculates on what football might really be all about.

I showed the almost completed book to a friend, a psychologist, and he said: "There are many people in here alone." It's true there is a lot of that; also there is a sense of solitude, and a lot of searching for something which probably means it's all about me.

What event do you remember most?

Of course it has to be The European Cup Final of 1985 in Brussels – the so-called Heysel disaster.

Like the players I went there to do a job, expecting it to be the same as a thousand times before – but unlike the players I ended up witnessing the most obscene tableau you can imagine and since then I have been living these images – it has coloured many things I have done afterwards. So 18 years later when this biography in photographs was suggested, how I would show the event was always going to be the one problem for me.

See this picture (*left*) – it shows the terrace, now it's no longer a mass of frightened people cowered by attack, it's a wasteland, it's just dreadful, bodies everywhere and all those loose shoes and the yellow airline bags.

Looking at this picture now is like coming to the event all over again, painfully treading up the terrace towards the medics, the police and what looked like firemen, and there it is on a hot evening in Brussels: the stadium before you, the grass bathed in the warm sun, and the dead in the blue shadows. Yet we worked on, I did what I was hired for and the players trudged off.

Thirty nine deaths at a football game as a result of British hooliganism is an outrage, a disgrace and whatever unease I may have about showing such a picture is overcome by the need for expressing why this can never be allowed to happen again.

Hooliganism is no longer a huge problem in English football. How has this figured in your work generally?

Although I detest hooliganism I have always been drawn to crowds as a subject but hardly ever to sporadic violence.

I suppose mass battles in the street or in the stadium on a grand scale are spectacular but very rare these days, however, when they do occur, it's hard to keep references from the films of Kurosawa or Eisenstein out of my mind.

Whatever photographic or cinematic "qualities" football violence may have though I would draw it out by thinking on the work of the humanist directors Chris Marker or Andre Tarkovsky, both of whom I particularly admire.

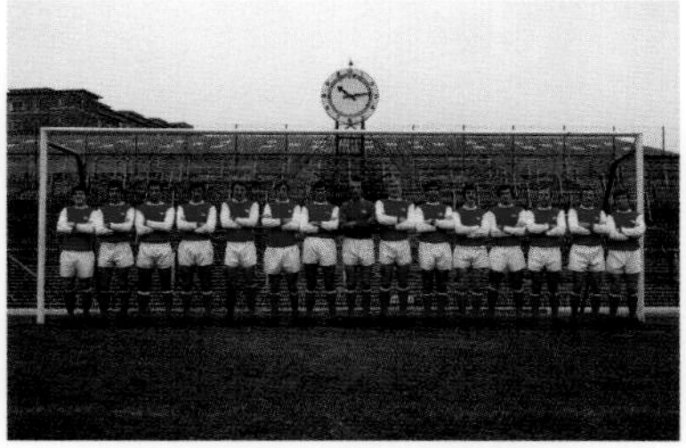

Arsenal FC
c 1969

Can you give some examples to show this process working?
Yes, there's a team picture of Scunthorpe from the '70s (*below and pp. 24–25*), but it's not the back-row, front-row stuff. It's taken on the terraces and you have 16 guys standing in a group wearing red shirts, red shorts and red socks and the point is, the kit has been washed so many times they are all different reds: the red of the shorts is different from the red of the shirts and some shirts are frayed and so on. And there is no badge and no signage, nothing apart from the group and the old-style terrace.

Right in the middle there is this guy who you sort of look at and think you might recognise, and of course it is Kevin Keegan. But we don't caption it that way. We don't try to point out this is Keegan, and that is intended because the picture is about the strip, not about Keegan. Next to the group we have a picture of Tony Book, the Manchester City captain from the great team of the late '60s. It's just a basic mugshot of him in the simple City sky-blue shirt with the white neckband. Both pictures are about a time not too long ago when football had simpler values.

It's clear after going through this editing process that with this book a chemical reaction of sorts has taken place, and what was originally just a collection of loosely bonded pictures may have become a new way of looking at football. At least I hope my work is viewed as idiomatic – hopefully you can't mistake my style for anyone else.

What does football mean to the world?
It's very important to many, and rightly so. It goes on whatever the circumstances. Even during appalling situations people can find time out from their problems to be together in a place that seems real but open to great possibilities of losing oneself in imagination – like the theatre. Sport I suppose is the lingua franca of our age, and the way it's sold to us nowadays through the media, particularly television, is rather interesting. One of my early influences, William Klein, was asked to give his views on the 2003 war on Iraq. He said: "I'm finding it hard to watch the war on American TV. It really drives me up the wall. You go from one basketball game to the other, one round-up of the basketball game and the best moments of the basketball game and a dunk competition – and then you go to the war, and they're talking exactly the same way: 'Hey, we're winning, we're going through.' And then they bring in analysts to talk about the war just like sports – it's all the same."

That's why I won't ever watch football on television. I prefer it when I am at the game or am going to the game. Once I am on my way then everything – whether it is the sight of something on the street that references the game or a newspaper headline or the colour of the sky – whatever it is I regard it all as material for a story. I don't see photography as just a window-like medium that describes the world "out there", that objectifies it – it can be a self-reflective process too, so maybe one could say 10,000 football matches have allowed me to have quite a few moments of self-reflection.

Tell me about some of the people you have photographed.
Bill Shankly (*pp. 99, 136–137*) was possibly the most stimulating man I ever photographed – even discussing how I might photograph him was a battle. I particularly liked the way he looked with his Rat Pack suits, his short-cropped hair and his pencil tie. Bill always looked cool, but he was actually a very warm man.

How has football changed since the 1960s?
Personally speaking, the photographic access I am given has changed dramatically in 30 years, for instance it has been impossible for me to photograph a Premier League game for seven years because I need a licence to work and the Premier League refuses to give me one. Apart from that the game is basically the same as it always was but with faster, fitter and maybe a greater number of skilful players. The packaging is a lot different, too, and television's influence is far-reaching, but football still has its usual cast of characters, reported on by a national media increasingly interested only in trivia.

Which photograph best sums up your style?
A difficult choice because in 38 years I have often changed my style. However, I would suggest the picture of Franco Baresi (*right and pp.342–343*) about to get his loser's medal in the 1994 World Cup Final, because although it has no recognisable visual style it does have a motif that I am drawn to again and again. I suppose as a composition it has all the elements: the cup is perfectly placed and there is a closed triangle relationship between it, the medal and Baresi; there is also a fourth element – the grinning hostess who hasn't read the moment or the mood – possibly she believes Italy have won.

I am like Baresi: dazzled by the presence of the cup, it looks so enticing that one could easily imagine it were solid gold. Yet Baresi steels himself to not look at it although it's only a metre or so away. He can't look at the medal either. Instead his eyes burn into [UEFA President Lennart] Johansson's, who appears to empathize with the predicament. And of course there is the medal – a pessimist's view would be it's offered like a noose for the neck, but I don't see it this way. Although it's only silver and offered limply in the Swede's rough workmanlike hands, it's presented like a precious object. There is great dignity in the picture: it's a defining moment. Although in football terms we know Baresi's a loser, possibly he is a winner in human terms. Either way, although it's a down moment I interpret it as an up. For me photography can never be just about facts and information – it's also about the photographer.

Interviewed by Nigel Atherton, June 2003

Scunthorpe United
c 1969

Tony Book
Manchester City captain
Maine Road 1968

Franco Baresi
1994 World Cup Final

STRIP

STRIP

Since the 1960s, when Peter Robinson began his career, changes in the design of football strips – once a rare phenomenon – have become the norm. This in turn has had an impact on the work of football photographers. Now the seasonal changes in strip design mean that stock photography has a shorter shelf-life – picture editors simply will not use a shot of a player unless he is wearing his team's latest strip. The replica market – a vitally important revenue stream for all professional clubs – needs to constantly re-jig strip design in order to stimulate demand on a season-by-season basis for what is essentially the same garment. Also, the great patrons of modern football – those who buy the right to put their names across the chests of footballers – have come to place great faith in the promotional possibilities of football strips – every professional football shirt is now a commercial billboard.

The football strip has not just been shaped by commercial culture, it has always reflected notions of popular fashion too. Before World War I football shirts were essentially button-up, long-sleeved white vests – the undergarments of the time – with bars, hoops and squares of contrasting colours. By the interwar years teams were beginning to appear in cotton drill shirts with collars and buttons. In 1958 English teams started to play in European competitions and this exposed the domestic game to the full impact of "continental" styling. V-necks, short sleeves and shorter shorts became features of the football costume during this period, as well as the inclusion of a club badge for the first time – this was often a re-working of a club's particular town or city corporate emblem.

During the 1960s, shirts changed in accordance with the prevailing "pop" aesthetic. The lines were simpler, less cluttered and more tubular. Necklines became circular, sleeves extended to the wrist and often the club badge was dispensed with altogether. Likewise traditional colour configurations took on bolder, geometric patterns, as if the whole ensemble had become a piece of Op Art. No doubt images of pop bands such as The Beatles and The Who, along with the generally Mod cut of youth fashions, influenced the development of strip design. Classic examples of this look were the 1960s' England and Manchester United strips with their clean lines and simple styling.

British football strips maintained the simple T-shirt look into the early 1970s until sportswear manufacturer Admiral began a series of bold strategic interventions in the appearance of the garment with their 1973 Leeds United strip. Their brash, mock-naval logo and trademark features such as long floppy collars and branded taping running the length of the shirt's sleeve, gave Admiral strips a distinctively flamboyant look that proved popular with clubs and fans. Soon the company became a dominant force in British football and its roster of clients grew to include the England national team, the Wales national team, Manchester United, Tottenham Hotspur, West Ham United and Southampton. It was during this decade that the three stripes of Franco-German sportswear manufacturers Adidas also made an appearance on the global stage. In the 1974 World Cup Finals Adidas supplied strips to a number of teams, but it was competition finalists Holland that caught the eye with their deep orange shirts set off by the Adidas stripes in stark black. Yet Robinson's photographs from the tournament show that one of the Dutch stars is not wearing an Adidas strip: close inspection of Johan Cruyff's kit reveals that his shirt has only two stripes.

In 1983 the English FA permitted the name or logo of a sponsor to be worn across the front of club shirts, thus opening up another area of the garment for visual exploitation. During the 1980s the application of surface patterning to football strips became a feature as pinstripes, contrasting colour panels and a host of other visual devices began to appear on football kits. While European strips maintained a degree of restraint, British football kit designs became increasingly flamboyant, and by the early 1990s the outfits had evolved into a riot of colours, patterns, motifs, trims and other superfluous features. It was at this time that replica shirts began to play an important part in the way football clubs generated money. This in turn led to clubs changing strip designs, both home and away, on a far more regular basis, thus mimicking seasonal cycles normally associated with Parisian couture houses. The strips became looser and more baggy; strange detail elements came and went – zips, buttons and drawstrings were all featured on necklines. British manufacturer Umbro became the major football brand of the 1990s: the England and Brazil national sides along with a host of top-flight clubs began to sport the company's "diamond" logo – Umbro's relationship with Manchester United, in particular, helped to drive sales of their products.

Today the manufacture of football strips has become a a global industry. During the 2002 World Cup in Japan and Korea it was clearly evident that US manufacturer Nike was now the brand leader in this lucrative market. In terms of style there now seems to be a move back to a more restrained design aesthetic.
The current generation of strips have begun to feature 1960s-style round necks and simpler colour configurations, with fibre and construction technologies now the driving forces behind an outfit's feel and appearance.

Peter Robinson's photographs provide a concise visual history of the way football strips have changed over time. They are no longer a simple dress code that differentiates one team from another: they have become an integral part of the economics of professional football. For example, the multi-million dollar transfer of Ronaldo from Inter Milan to Real Madrid in 2002 instantly secured massive sales of his new club strip across the world, thus offsetting some of his huge fee. ***Fd***

previous page

Twins, Ian and Roger Morgan
Queens Park Rangers
Loftus Road, London
1968

Frank Worthington
Huddersfield Town
1969

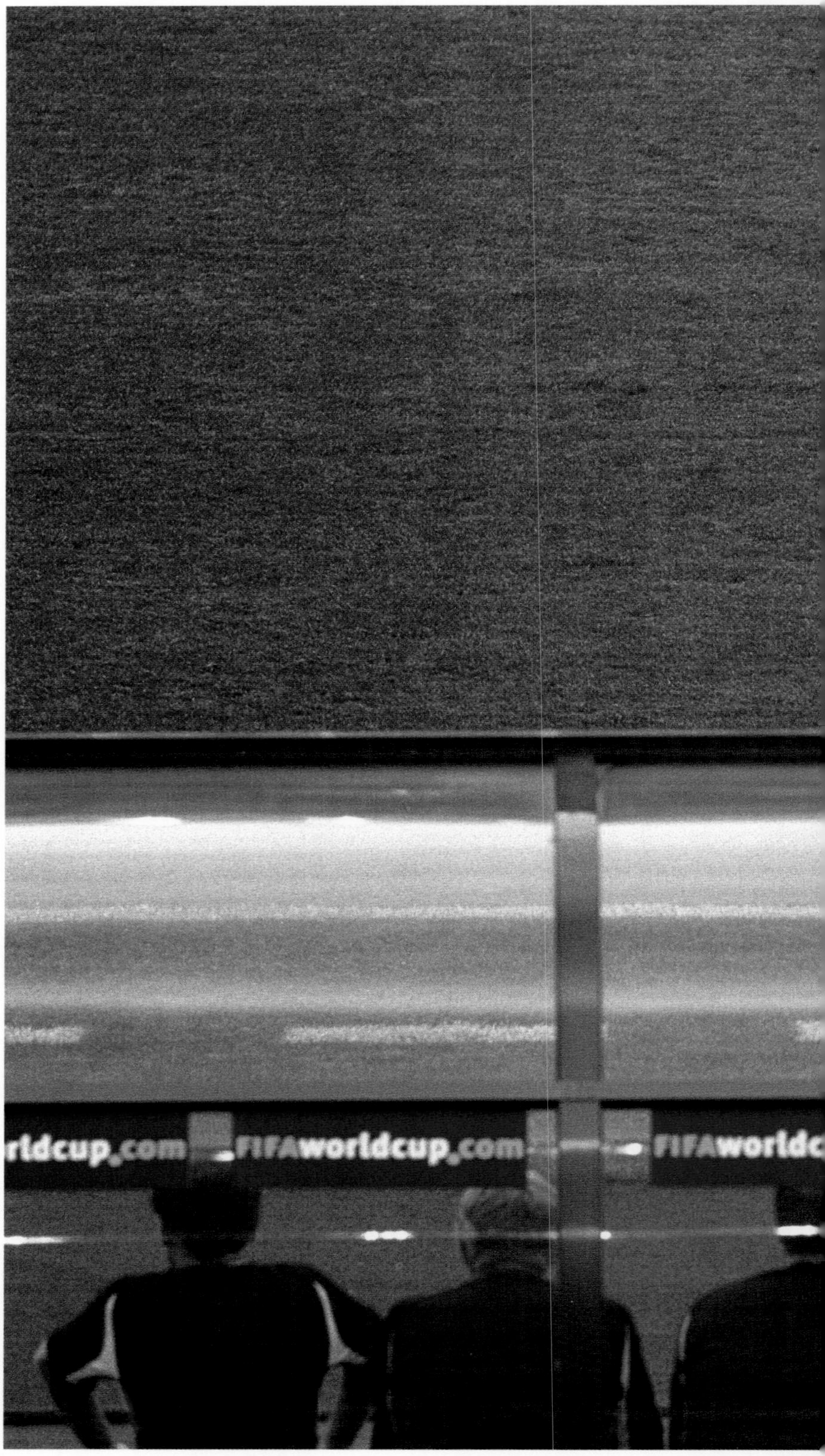

David Beckham
England v Nigeria
2002 World Cup
Osaka, Japan
16 June 2002

BECKHAM
7
FIFAworldcup.com
FIFAworldcup.com
FIFAworldcup.com

Malcolm Macdonald
Newcastle United
1971

Honved v Ferencvaros
Budapest, Hungary
March 1996

Mitre
MAESTRO
PERMAWHITE

previous page
Scunthorpe United
Home strip
c 1969

Tony Book
Manchester City captain
Maine Road
1968

Euro 2000, Brussels
Belgium v Turkey
Co-hosts Belgium exit
the tournament
19 June 2000

Japanese fans
In the subway en route to the
Turkey v Senegal Quarter-Final
2002 World Cup
Osaka, Japan
26 June 2002

USSR Team
Before friendly v Yugoslavia
1980s

previous page
George Best
Leeds United v
Manchester United
1968

England dressing room
Before 1990 World Cup
Semi-Final v West Germany
Turin, Italy
4 July 1990

Crystal

previous page
Johnny Byrne
Crystal Palace
1967

West Ham United
The defence (left to right):
Bobby Moore, John McDowell,
Tommy Taylor, Frank Lampard,
Bobby Ferguson, Billy Bonds.
The forwards (left to right):
John Ayris, Ronnie Boyce, Bryan
(Pop) Robson, Trevor Brooking,
Clyde Best, Harry Redknapp,
Geoff Hurst
1971

Trevor Francis, Roger Hynd and Bob Latchford
Sheffield United v
Birmingham City
Division Two
Bramall Lane
17 April 1971

BCFC
BCFC
BCFC
RH

Colin Todd, Sunderland
Roker Park
1968

following page
Liverpool
Before the FA Cup Final defeat
to Manchester United
11 May 1996

David Seaman
England v Bulgaria
Euro 2000 Qualifier
10 October 1998

RAVANELLI
11

CUP
1999

Northampton, England
Hanging out the Northampton Town team shirts in the garden c 1968

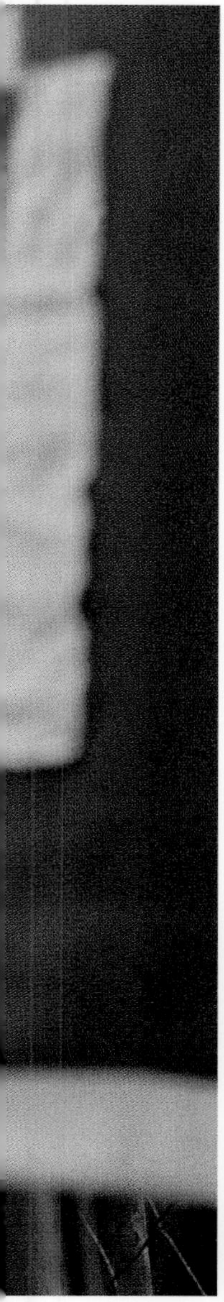

previous page
Fabrizio Ravanelli
Middlesbrough

Women's World Cup Final
USA v China
USA Women's team during the playing of The Stars and Stripes
Los Angeles
10 July 1999

2002 World Cup Semi-Final
Brazil v Turkey
Saitama, Japan
26 June 2002

Watford
umbro

12

previous page

Watford v Aston Villa

Luther Blissett and Allan Evans. The Watford shirt sponsor is hidden from the BBC TV cameras due to advertising restrictions
19 February 1983

1992 Olympics, Barcelona

Ghana goalkeeper with hastily customized substitute shirt
7 August 1992

Watney Cup Final

The Baseball Ground
Derby County v Manchester United
8 August 1970

PALE
ST ALE

West Germany v Albania
1984 European Championship qualifier. The Germans in traditional three-striped Adidas shirts include Rummenigge, Voeller and Littbarski. The Albanians (who scored first but lost 2-1) sport a unique four-stripe kit of their own design
Kaiserslautern
20 November 1983

Honduras v Mexico
World Cup Qualifier
Tegucigalpa
22 November 1981

Ghana team
FIFA Under 17 World
Championships
10 June 1989

Birmingham City v Liverpool
5 May 1984

Michel Platini
Juventus v Avellino
Turin, Italy
8 September 1985

Herbie the Hammer
West Ham United mascot
c 2000

following page
1974 World Cup
Johan Cruyff in his
famousNo 14 shirt
Holland v Bulgaria
Dortmund, West Germany
23 June 1974

Johan Cruyff
Wearing Barcelona change kit

14
20

HOME

30P 6d ENCLOSURE
65P 13/- STAND
CHARLT
Evening Standard
CHARLTON

ON ATHLETIC
30p
ENCLOSUR
FLOYD ROAD, S.E.7.
LILLIAN BOARD

HOME

In response to the tragedies at Bradford in 1985 and Hillsborough in 1989, British football grounds went through a period of architectural redevelopment on an unprecedented scale. These two events had focused attention on the fact that crowd safety was being all but ignored as grounds developed in a vernacular fashion with "improvements" being made as and when required. Surprisingly these issues had not arrived out of the blue – there was a history to these problems. Government reports into crowd behaviour and safety had been produced on a fairly regular basis – the Shortt Report in 1924, the Molewyn Hughes Report in 1946, the Chester Report in 1966, the Harrington Report in 1968, the Lang Report in 1969, the Wheatley Report in 1972, the McElhone Report in 1977, the Department of the Environment report into crowd behaviour at football grounds in 1984 and the Popplewell Report in 1986. In all, nine major studies into various aspects of behaviour and safety at British football grounds that pre-dated the Taylor Report.

So much redevelopment of the game's architectural fabric has since occurred that it is hard to imagine the relatively ungoverned spaces in which the game used to be played. To the modern eye the grounds that form the backdrop to many of Robinson's photographs appear almost semi-derelict and brutal in their design. Another aspect that stands out in Robinson's photography from the pre-Taylor era is the proximity of industry and manufacture to many British stadiums. Of course, professional football grew out of 19th century urban-industrial culture, but it is still startling to see how tight that bond was – as is apparent from the factory chimneys and rows of terraced housing that form the horizons in many of the images. Photographs of fans shoehorned into tight and claustrophobic spaces are another reminder of how football grounds had evolved as places of containment, a design aesthetic that was closer to prison architecture than a sports ground. Robinson's photographs stand as a testament to the good old/bad old days of British football.

Before the 1990s, images of football from Europe and South America seemed to come from a different planet. The stadiums always appeared so much grander, so much bigger – the San Siro, the Nou Camp, the Maracana, the Bernabeu, the Azteca – tier upon tier of cantilevered stands reaching up and up, graceful curves sweeping around in architectural unity, these constructions appeared more like giant UFOs than football grounds. And the crowds – eighty, ninety, one hundred thousand–plus capacities. In comparison the sheds and terraces that characterized many British football grounds appeared parochial and ugly, like some kind of embarrassing provincial cousin. Even the layout of the standard British football ground seemed unsophisticated and clumsy; blocks placed corner to corner in a rectilinear ground plan, a basic layout system that had been in place since the days of Archibald Leitch, the founding father of British stadium design. Of course, the images being mediated back were only offering glimpses of prestige grounds and, as Heysel proved, Britain did not have a monopoly on crumbling and dangerous stadiums. Yet the impression given by many of Robinson's British photographs from the 1980s is still of a game in decline with an architectural fabric to match.

The Italia '90 World Cup Finals offered Britain a tantalizing glimpse of what could be – football played by superstars in architect-designed stadiums. It threw into sharp relief the decaying state of the British football environment, but the images beamed back from the continent also suggested that the seemingly intractable problems of hooliganism, disasters and the sheer parochialism of football in Britain could simply be sidestepped by repackaging the sport – as the Taylor Report pointed out, connections could be made between shoddy grounds and poor behaviour. Of course vast sums needed to be spent and these became available – at least to top-flight teams – through the sale of British football to Sky Television. Add to that government grants made available through the Football Trust and by the early 1990s the Great Leap Forward was under way.

In an interview at about this time a football executive explained the rationale behind his club's proposed relocation from its historic inner-city ground to an all-new, purpose-built stadium on the outskirts. He explained that the club's core audience no longer lived in the area. Now it was time to take flight themselves and a new future beckoned that would involve retail concessions, function rooms and fast food outlets. "Just like with cinemas," he went on, "the flea pit is dead. People want a clean, multi-functional leisure facility and we can't offer them this at our present ground." The ground in question had had a long and honourable history: championships had been won there, some of the top European sides had visited and a host of great players had performed on the pitch. But times were changing, and the club's response was ambitious and forward-looking. In their present situation they felt left behind, like a strange relic of a bygone era.

Since that interview the club has moved away from the derelict factories and back-to-back housing to a new stadium at the centre of a business park. Its new neighbours include call centres, internet banking firms, out-of-town supermarkets – titans of the post-industrial economy. And in a way this club, and others that have made similar moves, have come full circle. The decline in British football mirrored the decline in the old industrial order – decay, neglect and a history of confrontation. The new sunshine industries trading in communications and retail are the 21st-century patrons of football and they have brought us suburban stadiums, multi-functional stadiums for the new leisure age. ***Fd***

previous page
The Valley, London SE7
c 1970

Filbert Street, Leicester
1967

EURO 2000
FUJIFILM
McDonald's
JVC

www.euro2000.org
JVC HI-FI & VIDEO
JVC
adidas
Adecco
nashuatec

previous page
Amsterdam Arena
Holland v France
Euro 2000
21 June 2000

Whaddon Road, Cheltenham
Cheltenham Town v Rochdale
Cheltenham's first game in the Football League
7 August 1999

Victoria Ground, Stoke
1997

Yokohama, Japan
2002 World Cup Final venue

Somerton Park, Newport
Home of Newport County, then a Football League club, now in the Dr Martens Premier League

Sapporo Dome, Japan
Italy's Christian Vieri opens the scoring against Ecuador at the only indoor venue of the 2002 World Cup
3 June 2002

England v Germany
The last game at Wembley is a 1-0 defeat for an England team managed by Kevin Keegan (just visible here as he walks past the goal). He resigned immediately afterwards
7 October 2000

Mitre
adidas
Nationwide
BURTON
AXA
EIDOS EIDOS
WALKERS WALKERS
one 2 one
Nationwide
Sainsbury's
Nationwide
WALKERS WALKERS
Coca-Cola
Coca-Cola
EIDOS EIDOS
AXA

City Ground, Nottingham
Nottingham Forest v
Birmingham City
29 April 1978

Boothferry Park
The stadium Hull City left
for good in 2003

BERMiTZ

The Reebok Stadium, Bolton
Bolton Wanderers' new home
in the suburbs
April 2002

Stotfold FC, Bedfordshire
A preliminary round game in
the FA Cup
21 August 1999

12
1
2
3
4
5
6
7
8
9
10
11

The Clock End, Highbury
Arsenal team c 1969

Leyton Pennant v Wembley
FA Cup Extra Preliminary
Qualifying Round
5 August 1998

Hillsborough, Sheffield
FA Cup Semi-Final Replay
Middlesbrough supporters put up with a restricted view of the game v Chesterfield
22 April 1997

euro2000.org
FUJIFILM
McDonald's
HYUNDAI
PHILIPS
Carlsberg
Carlsberg
Coca-Cola enjoy
PHILIPS

The Baseball Ground, Derby
Derby County Championship celebrations 1975

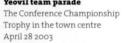

previous page
Germany v Romania
Liège, Belgium
Euro 2000
12 June 2000

Porto FC, Portugal
Ticket window

Yeovil team parade
The Conference Championship
Trophy in the town centre
April 28 2003

The Angel of the North
Antony Gormely's landmark
statue near Gateshead

Seoul 1988
Italy v West Germany
Olympic Tournament Final

Burnden Park, Bolton
The terraces fill for the last time
25 April 1997

Bootham Crescent, York
York City v Wycombe Wanderers
Passers-by enjoy a kickabout as the match ball comes over the wall during the game

Oakwell, Barnsley
En route to promotion to
the Premier League
1998

Goodison Park, Everton
The Church of St Luke the Evangelist in the corner of the ground, with the Gladwys Street End to the right
c 1971

A B C D E F G H
BENSON and HEDGES

Filbert Street, Leicester
Leicester City's final game at Filbert Street v Tottenham Hotspur
11 May 2002

London 2000
Tribute to the Millwall player of the '60s and '70s

FFORESTFACH TEL 32599

CHESTERFIELD
FOOTBALL CLUB LTD
LETTERS
REGISTERED OFFICE.
SOLD OUT

Accrington, Lancashire
Peel Park, defunct home of former Football League Club Accrington Stanley

previous page
Vetch Field, Swansea
Railway sleepers serve as terraces for Swansea City

Chesterfield
Demand overwhelms supply as a surge in interest accompanies Chesterfield's run to the Semi-Finals of the 1997 FA Cup

Victoria Ground, Stoke
Supporters leave Stoke City's ground for the last time, helping themselves to souvenirs
4 May 1997

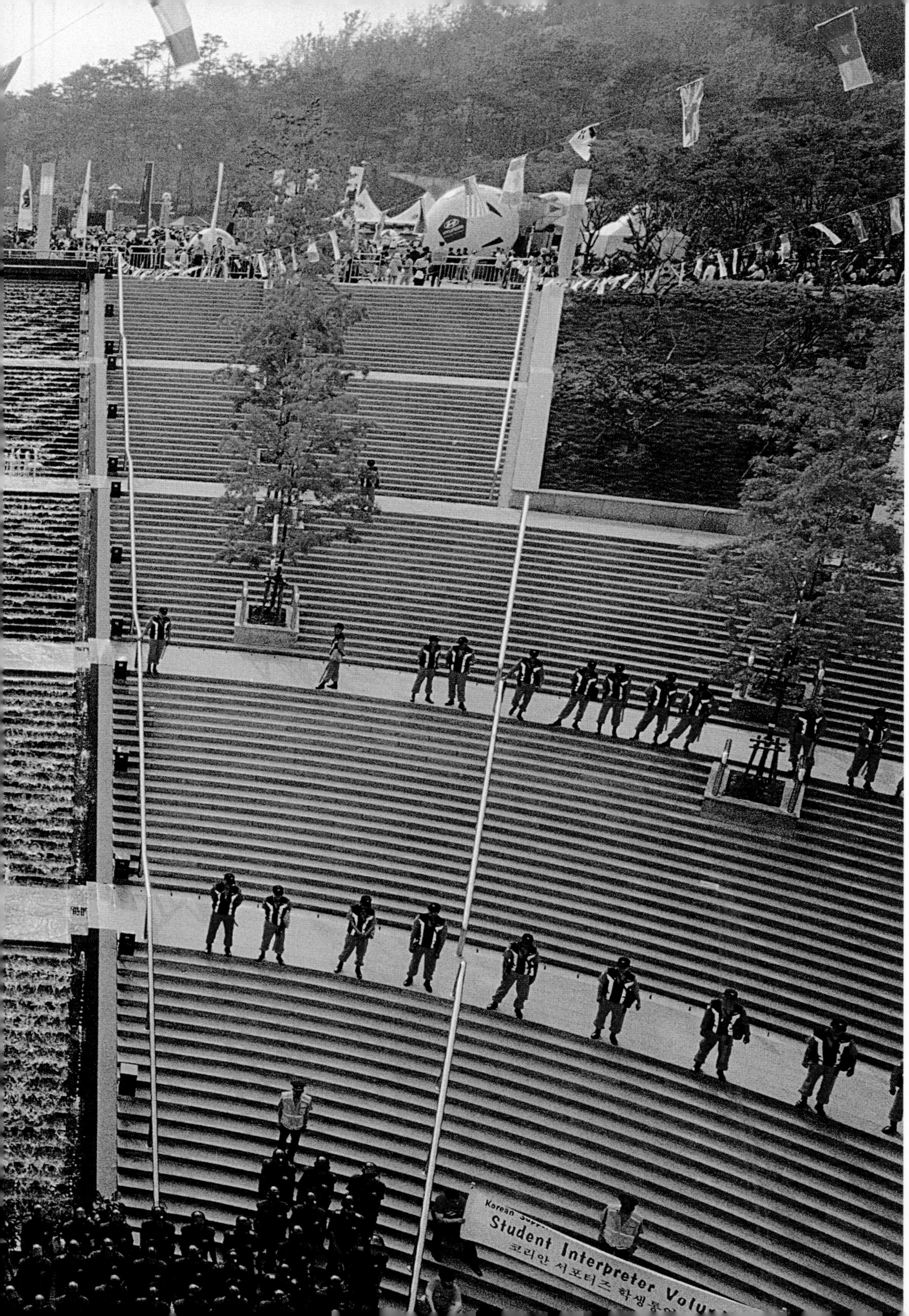

Opening game, 2002 World Cup
France v Senegal
Seoul Stadium, South Korea
31 May 2002

TOUCHLINE

LAND

TOUCHLINE

The brooding presence on the touchline is a key football image, the manager glaring at the drama unfolding before him, ultimately responsible for the outcome yet unable to intervene beyond reshuffling the playing pack. To the outsider it is a strange and enigmatic role: after all most of the manager's work is done behind closed doors – conferring with the board, trading in the transfer market, overseeing training, discussing tactics and team selection with backroom staff, dealing with players in the privacy of the changing room. Yet come matchday managers become principal players and like ringmasters at the circus their role is emblematic not active, choreographing, cajoling, part of yet apart from the action – conductor, cheerleader and commander all rolled into one. And both television and the print media rely on shots of managers to act as vehicles to suggest an array of emotions that a team might be feeling – joy, sorrow, despair, hope, celebration, anxiety. Unlike footballers who are wrapped up in actually playing during a match, the manager is on the sidelines acting out the various trigger points as they occur. The manager, apart from his coaching duties, also plays a highly visual role during the course of a football match.

Peter Robinson's career as a football photographer has brought him into contact with some of the game's most celebrated managers – Ramsey, Menotti, Bearzot, Beckenbauer, Zagalo and Schoen have all been captured within his viewfinder. And, as with other areas of his work, the nature of management has undergone fundamental changes during the years he has been covering the game. Managers used to be the conduit through which the board governed the club. They suggested the team, but the board made the final selection. In England this situation was still evident with the managership of the national side into the 1960s. Walter Winterbottom, Sir Alf Ramsey's predecessor, still had to take his team sheet to the FA for their approval. A poor run of results starting with Hungary's 6-3 defeat of England at Wembley in an exhibition match, and indifferent form in the 1958 and 1962 World Cup finals led the English FA to relinquish their role as national team selectors and instead allowed Ramsey to fulfil the modern-day role of manager as team supremo.

In England the league clubs had been quicker to adapt to having managers who performed the role of both figurehead and decision-maker. Herbert Chapman had run first Huddersfield Town then Arsenal as personal fiefdoms during the inter-war years, and the post-war period had seen the emergence of charismatic and innovative managers such as Stan Cullis, Arthur Rowe, Bill Nicholson, Matt Busby and, slightly later, Bill Shankly. By the start of Robinson's career Busby was the grand old man of British football and Shankly was beginning to shape Liverpool into a force that would dominate English football for years to come. Robinson photographed Shankly on many occasions: what was his impression of the man? Surprisingly aware and conscious of his public image is Robinson's verdict. Although Shankly liked to present himself to the media as a no-nonsense disciplinarian, in private he gave glimpses of a far more complex personality, Machiavellian even. Robinson felt that Shankly used his Scottishness, or at least the English media's preconceptions of Scottishness, to reinforce a dour image of himself – a tactic that gave him an aura of someone to be reckoned with, someone to be frightened of. By contrast Robinson found that Busby, another Scot, projected himself as warm and approachable, someone who had your interests at heart, an almost grandfatherly figure. But Robinson heard through the football grapevine that Busby was just as capable as Shankly of imposing his will.

During the 1970s Robinson also came into regular contact with the two emergent titans of English football, Don Revie and Brian Clough. Again, like Shankly and Busby, they deliberately constructed public personae to manage their relations with their players and the press. For Clough this was a messianic characterisation, somebody who could manage football teams, indeed manage anything, through sheer willpower and force of personality. Revie, on the other hand, liked to present himself as the quiet schemer, the master tactician who compiled dossiers on the opposition and wherever possible attempted to reduce the odds by careful scientific planning. The clash of these two styles was made evident in their joint appearance on BBC Television's *Michael Parkinson Show*. Clough, savvy to the demands of the broadcast media and finely attuned to the value of a good soundbite, was the master of the occasion, throwing out lines and producing snappy responses to questions. Revie was left in his wake, desperately trying to explain subtle tactical nuances and unable to turn the occasion to his advantage. Clough knew how to make contact with the audience beyond the studio and in response people loved to see "Old Big Head" doing his stuff. Yet the Robinson collection is rich in images of Revie during his time at Leeds United and one assumes from this that the manager must have recognised the value of allowing the photographer to get close to him and his squad of players.

Looking through Robinson's images of managers, one is struck by the intimacy of many of the shots – strange off-duty tableaux, enigmatic portraits, quizzical glances and oddly banal moments frozen in time. Away from the dugout, most of these men appear oddly normal, and resemble nothing so much as unfashionable relatives – all Gannex raincoats and slip-on shoes. Perhaps these images contain the real truth: that these are just ordinary company men who for 90 minutes a week don the mantle of giants. ***Fd***

previous page
Sven-Goran Eriksson
England coach
England v Sweden
2002 World Cup

Bill Shankly
Liverpool manager
The staff canteen at Anfield
1959–74

Bertie Mee
The man behind the first Arsenal League and Cup double in 1971

Tommy Docherty
Manchester United manager
Leeds United v
Manchester United
Elland Road
c 1975

ABCDE

previous page
Matt Busby
Manchester United manager, with trainer Jack Crompton
c 1968

Bill Nicholson
Tottenham Hotspur manager in his office at White Hart Lane
c 1967

Stewart Houston
The temporary manager of Arsenal after the sacking of George Graham, Houston sits in the Highbury directors' box wearing the club's strip
1995

Franz Beckenbauer
West Germany manager
1990 World Cup
Italy

INTER CLUB SAVONA
FIAT
Coca-Cola
Voltaren Emulgel
GEIGY

Johan Cruyff
Barcelona manager
Barcelona v Juventus
European Cup Winners Cup
Semi-Final 1st leg
Nou Camp
10 April 1991

Rinus Michels
Holland manager (below right), Cruyff's mentor, with assistant manager Dick Advocaat
Holland v Germany
1992 European Championship
Gothenburg, Sweden
18 June 1992

Michel Hidalgo
France coach (head down, seated)
seconds from victory in 1984
European Championship Final
Paris, France
27 June 1984

previous page
Don Revie
Chelsea v Leeds United
1970 FA Cup Final
Leeds captain Billy Bremner (far left) catches his manager's eye at the opposite end of the line-up Wembley
11 April 1970

Alex Ferguson
Manchester United manager with his captain Bryan Robson
European Cup Winners Cup Final v Barcelona
Rotterdam, Holland
15 May 1991

Carlos Bilardo
England v Argentina
1986 World Cup
Mexico City
22 June 1986

ARG 2 ENG 0
JVC
SANTA
PARA SEGUIR
AVANZANDO

Enzo Bearzot
Italy manager
Buenos Aires, Argentina
1977

Joe Mercer and Bill Shankly
Managers of Manchester City
and Liverpool
Anfield
12 January 1971

Alan Ball
During his first stint as Portsmouth manager (1984–89). He returned to the club in 1998–99

previous page
Harry Catterick
The Everton manager (far right) prepares his team for extra time
v West Bromwich Albion
1968 FA Cup Final
Wembley
18 May 1968

Bobby Robson
England coach
Greece v England
Athens
17 November 1982

Jack Charlton
Ireland coach as his team lose to host nation Italy in 1990 World Cup Quarter-Final
Rome
30 June 1990

Ali Chatali
Tunisia manager as his team prepare to celebrate qualification for the 1978 World Cup
Tunis

Danny Blanchflower
Republic of Ireland v
Northern Ireland
The Northern Ireland coach
shakes hands with Johnny Giles
as Northern Ireland's Martin
O'Neill passes
Dublin
20 September 1978

Don Revie (right) and Les Cocker
Everton v Leeds United
Goodison Park
c 1972

previous page
Brian Clough and his players
The Baseball Ground
Derby
c 1969

Jack Charlton
Middlesbrough manager
Everton v Middlesbrough
c 1975

adidas

Nationwide
Bodycote

previous page
Bobby Robson
The Ipswich Town manager enjoys a pre-match meal before an away game against Wolverhampton Wanderers
c 1980

Sammy McIlroy
Macclesfield Town manager during the club's first League game v Torquay United
9 August 1997

Malcolm Allison
The Manchester City manager (in white coat) in the stands at Maine Road. Behind him is Joe Mercer
c 1969

Matt Busby
Manchester United manager
Old Trafford
c 1968

previous page
Helmut Schoen
West Germany manager with his captain Franz Beckenbauer after his team beat Holland 2–1 in 1974 World Cup Final
Olympic Stadium, Munich
7 July 1974

Bill Shankly
Liverpool manager in the year the club won its eighth League Championship and its first European honour, the UEFA Cup
April 1973

FAN

8

FAN

Fans give football its rich pageant, its festival, its sounds and even its smells – without an audience football ceases to be theatre. Football fans can be frightening too – kicking, smashing, fighting, destroying, hurting. By the 1980s in Britain football fans had become a problem: they were people who needed containing, caging in, identifying. But how had this state of affairs come about?

As with so many aspects of football culture, the precedents go back a surprisingly long way. Accounts of rowdy and even violent behaviour at football matches can be traced to the late 19th century. Local toughs such as the Peaky Blinders from Birmingham would ally themselves to football teams and attack opposition fans and players. The impact of social, cultural and economic changes in the decades after World War II helped to create the conditions for a re-emergence of football hooliganism – a more urbanized population, a high birth rate, increased disposable incomes for young people and the crossover influence of youth subcultures such as Teddy Boys, Mods and Rockers. The emergence of skinheads as the epitome of terrace "yob" dates from this period and their "look" in many ways parodied Victorian working-class dress – heavy boots, braces and half-mast trousers. Perhaps it was this combination of massed ranks of young men, dressed in a uniform manner that made the hooligan problem appear to be far more widespread than it actually ever was. The reality is that most football fans, then and now, go to matches for all the right reasons – to enjoy the spectacle, to be part of the theatre of the occasion and for the pleasure of being absorbed into the crowd. Anecdotal evidence suggests that for many young male football fans the "look" was simply that, a dress code that connected you with your peers and showed a certain sartorial awareness. The right brand of jeans and the particular haircut were far more important than fighting: it was more about looking "hard" than being "hard". However by the mid-1980s in the aftermath of the Heysel Stadium riots the reputation of English football fans reached its nadir, and the basic equation that football fans equal trouble was set in stone.

But a new fan culture emerged during the 1980s, one that used creativity, wit and comment as weapons, a culture that gave fans an independent voice and sought to reclaim the debate about football and football fans. Its chosen medium was the fanzine. These home-produced magazines devoted to particular clubs offered all the opportunities that the "official" media could not – irreverence, offbeat humour and an independent voice for the fan. An inherent problem of the relationship between professional football clubs and the media is that self-regulation is exercised by both sides to protect mutual benefits – nobody rocks the boat too much because clubs can deny access and papers can print negative stories. The fanzines were beholden to no one, not reliant on advertising revenue or access to the stars and so obviously out of the loop that they could claim authority through credibility. Also, and as a result of the Hillsborough disaster in 1989, the Football Supporters Association and other fan-based pressure groups emerged to counter the charge that all football fans were potential, if not actual, hooligans. Fans were simply refusing to be typecast: they organized pressure groups, created an alternative media and took an active part in debates about professional football.

Italia '90 was meant to be the endgame for English football – a bad reputation, a history of trouble and the fact that so many fans would be able to travel to Italy spelt disaster. But a combination of strict policing, alcohol bans and a determination not to conform to type turned expectations on their head and for once the England fans, in the main, decided to party instead of rioting. The transformation this tournament had on the status of English football fans cannot be understated – irony and humour replaced violence and intolerance, and the world's press witnessed it all. In England the new mood created by the success of Italia '90 and a raft of government legislation aimed at controlling the football environment combined to create a different fan culture. CCTV technology and the revamping of many of the country's stadiums created a safer, more controllable environment. Meanwhile new initiatives set out to eradicate racist chanting and racist behaviour. For many years the clubs, the FA and the media had simply ignored such issues, and showed little interest in acknowledging there was a problem, never mind doing something about it. Fans, with the assistance of government, the football establishment and players themselves, demanded an end to racism in football – as a result it is now rare for matches to be marred by racist abuse and chanting. Indeed, the way the FA and English clubs tackled the problems became something of a blueprint that other countries may follow to eradicate their own troublesome elements. There is a dark irony in the fact that hooliganism – the so-called "English Disease" – has been such a successful British export that it has now become a European problem.

As football has re-financed itself so the relationship between fans and clubs has changed. The array of goods and services that clubs offer their fans has caused a subtle shift – higher prices, greater levels of merchandising, share options and an emphasis on football as a market-driven leisure activity have imposed a quasi-client status on fans. And since the customer is always right, we may be entering a phase in professional football in which it is acknowledged that the real commercial muscle belongs to the fans. If this is the age of the consumer-led democracy then those who buy into the game, be they regular match-goers, armchair fans or minor shareholders, have the power to shape their game. ***Fd***

previous page
Sunderland v Arsenal
FA Cup Semi-Final
Hillsborough, Sheffield
7 April 1973

Rivaldo and Ronaldo
2002 World Cup Final
Yokohama, Japan
30 June 2002

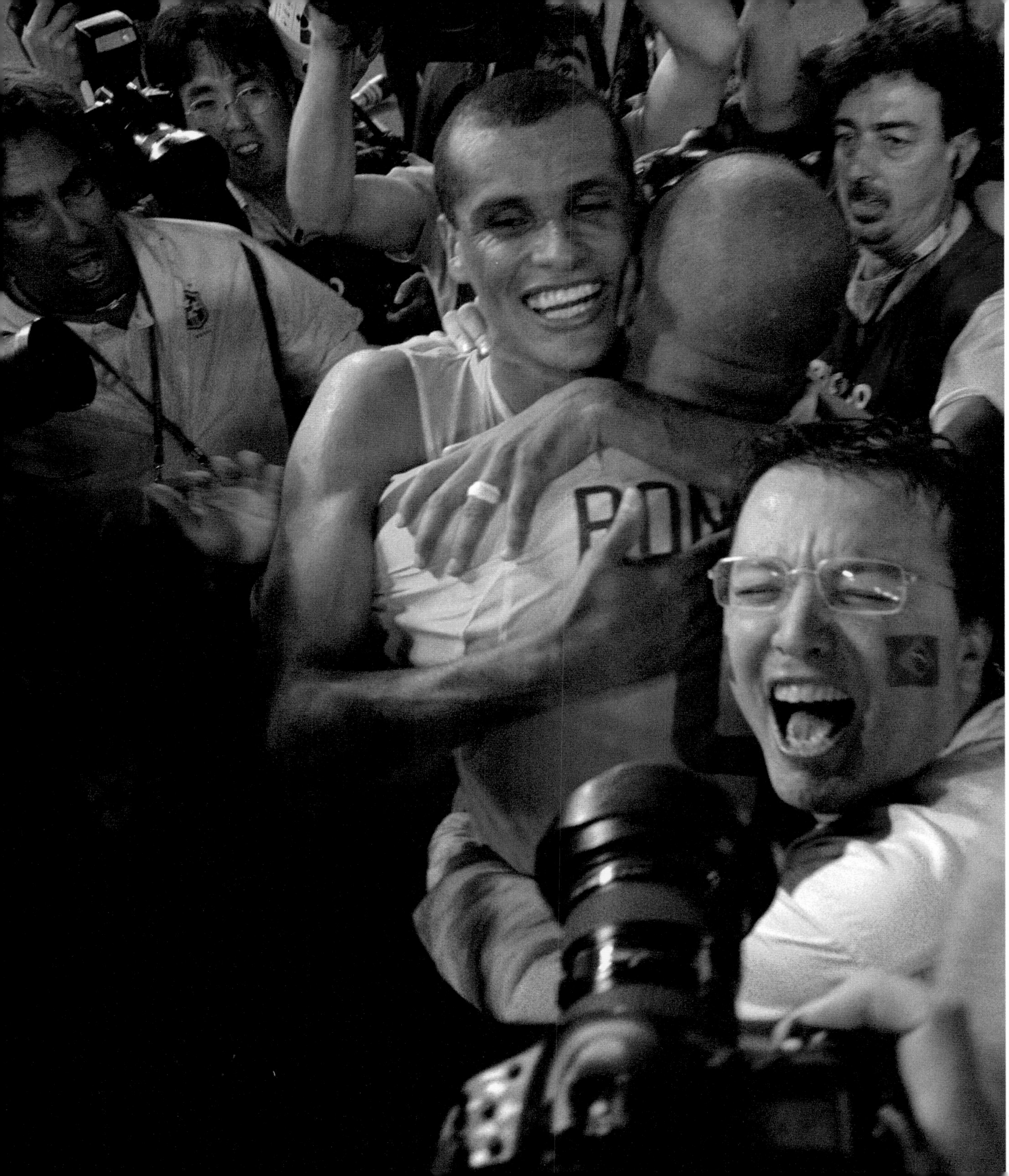

Leeds United v
Manchester United
FA Cup Semi-Final
Hillsborough, Sheffield
14 March 1970

Barnet Football Club, London
Barnet v Torquay United
Barnet's final game in the
Football League
5 May 2001

Croatia supporters celebrate victory over Italy
2002 World Cup
Ibaraki, Japan
8 June 2002

Anfield Road End, Liverpool
c 1972

Tottenham Hotspur wall
Manchester c 1972

to phone
your friends?
After six
and
at weekends.
GPO
The Phone Service is
moving forward
VOTE
X Conservative
MPS
1364
JENNINGS
BEAL
KINNEAR
ENGLAND
CHIVERS
GILZEAN
VENABLES
GREAVES
ODEON
Baby Love
ISLE of MAN
motor cycle RACES
TT 100 MGP
OMAR SHARIF · CATHERINE DENEUVE · JAMES MASON · AVA GARDNER
MAYERLING
ABC DEANSGATE

トイレ

Yokohama FC supporters
Shizuoka, Japan
December 1999

Clarence Park, St Albans City
FA Cup 1st Round
30 October 1999

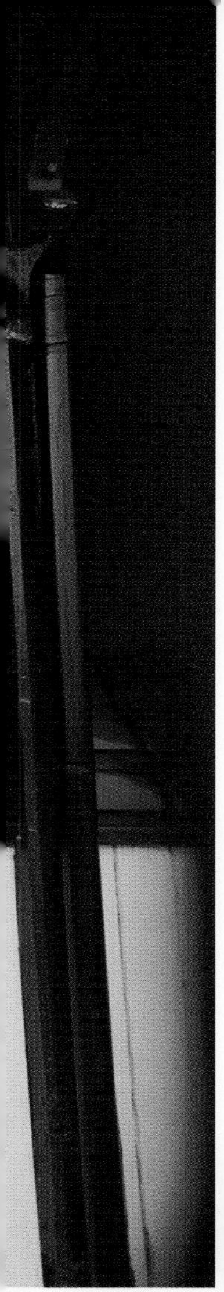

Aston Villa v Ipswich Town
When it was still possible to
see part of the pitch from
Aston Park
14 April 1981

Manchester City supporters
Macclesfield Town v
Manchester City
Worthington Cup
8 September 1998

Nationwide

Manchester Evening News
football PINK
FIRST with results & reports
TARTAN Beer

Rodney Marsh
First game for Manchester City v Chelsea
18 March 1972

Brugge, Belgium
May 2000

following page
Lomé, Republic of Togo
April 1981

Odori Park, Sapporo, Japan
Six hours before England
play Argentina
7 June 2002

Roma supporters
European Cup Final v Liverpool
Rome, Italy
30 May 1984

European Cup Final
Belgian riot police baton charge
against Liverpool supporters
Heysel Stadium,
Brussels, Belgium
29 May 1985

TOILETS
REFRESHMENTS

EVENING LEADER

previous page
Goal by Cambridge
Wrexham v Cambridge United
FA Cup 4th round
8 January 2000

Dennis Bergkamp cut-out
1998 World Cup
Marseille, France

Belgium v Ireland
Republican banners protest against Maze prison H Blocks
March 1981

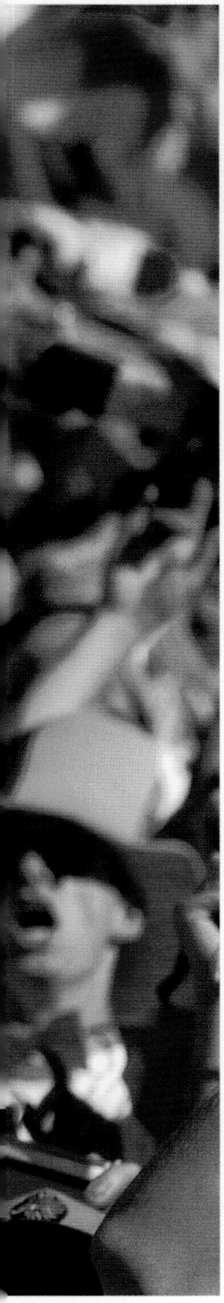

TALCO
SODORANTE OSSART
OSSART
RE KINO ¡ ué padre vino !

Brazil player throws shirt to the crowd
Mexico City
June 1983

Hampden Park, Glasgow
Scotland v England
25 May 1985

Manchester United fans
FA Cup Final
Wembley
18 May 1985

Japan supporters
2002 World Cup
Osaka, Japan

Nigeria supporters
Railway station, Nantes, France
1998 World Cup

和歌山
JR
質・買取
質
いづみや
6691-4144
長居公園

Bamber supporters
St Albans City v Bamber Bridge
St Albans, Hertfordshire
FA Cup 1st Round, 1999

GIORGIO
BAX

Pat Jennings
Tottenham Hotspur training ground, Cheshunt
c 1973

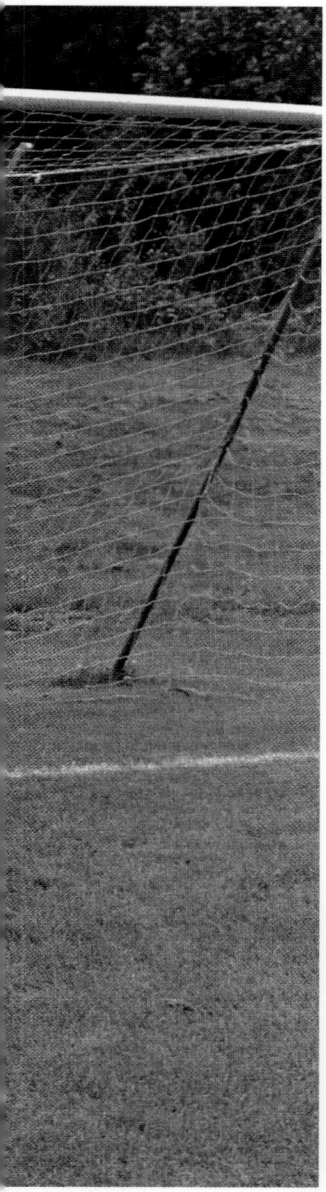

The North Bank
Arsenal v Sheffield Wednesday
29 August 1992

Marlboro
SMART!
GMB UNION
GMB UNION
ATARI FANATIC ATARI

Griffin Park
Brentford v Derby County
FA Cup 3rd Round
4 January 2003

PITCH

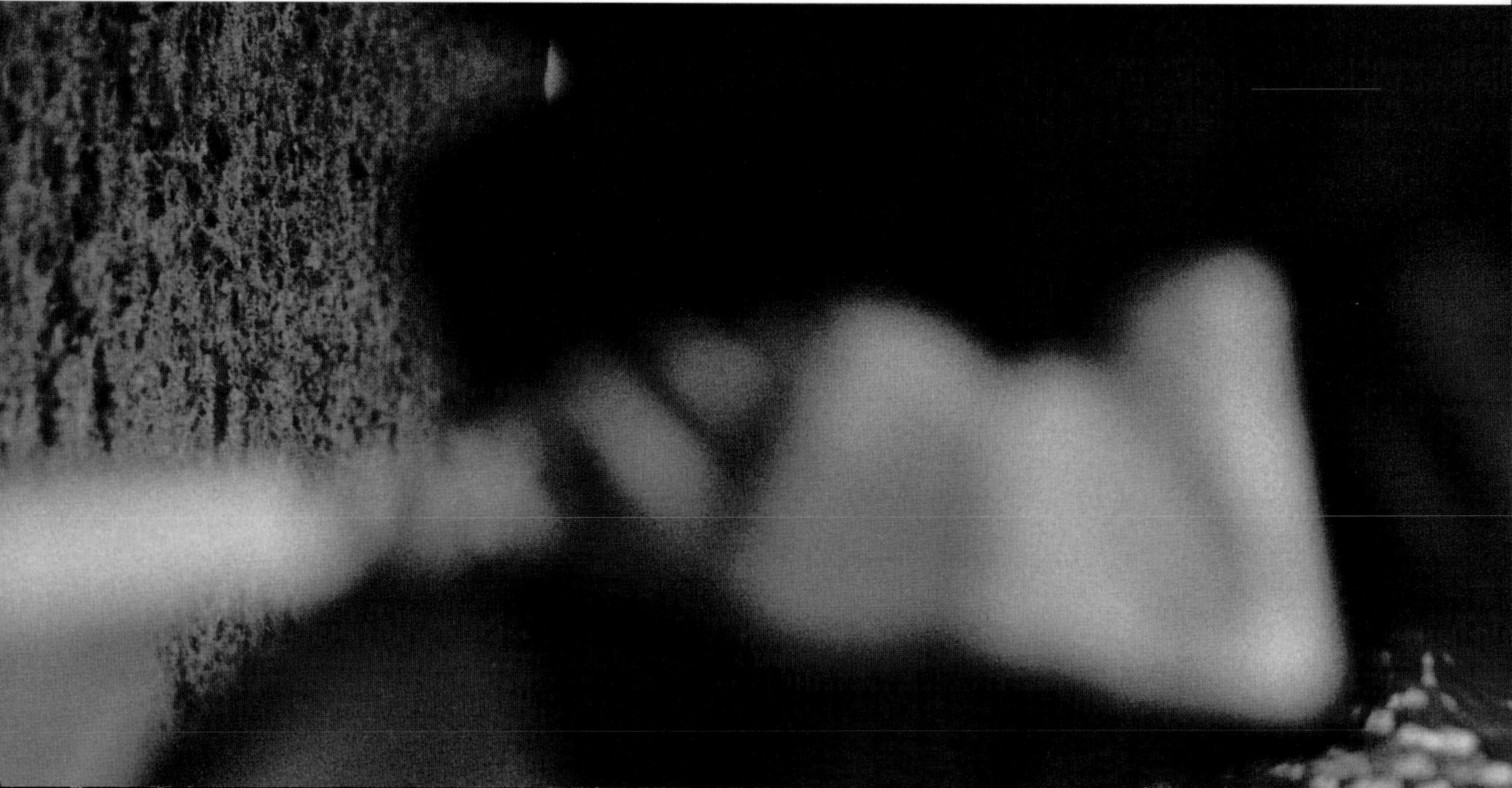

SCORERS

PITCH

Action is the stock-in-trade of the sports photographer – the goal, the save, the foul. For the snapper it is all about getting the "money shot", the image that is going to appear across the back pages the following morning. The football photographer's area of operations is pitch-side with the two penalty areas always covered, ready for goalmouth scrambles, shots and saves. The photo pack is made up of staffers (those employed by a specific newspaper or magazine), club photographers (producing images for a club's own use), agency photographers (working for independent agencies who sell on images to media outlets) and freelancers (one-man bands who may be commissioned for a particular assignment). The photographer will also be looking for player-stock (single player portraits), images of general action, perhaps some stadium and fan shots, and anything that catches the eye and could be sold for further editorial use. Images that tell the story of particular matches – the photos that appear in the next day's papers – usually have a relatively short life. They have an immediate value in that they illustrate match reports, but that is often the only use that is made of them.

Peter Robinson has been a staffer, worked for photo-agencies and, for the bulk of his professional life, operated as a freelancer. Because of this independent status the Robinson archive contains a richness and variety of images that would not have been accumulated had he spent a career simply going for the money shot. Also, Robinson's obsessive mapping of the football event has meant he has produced images that, at the time, would simply not have had any secondary commercial value. Many of the images featured in the collection go beyond functional reportage – blurred figures in the foreground, noir-ish camera angles and anonymous faces peering out of the crowd are just a few of the "less commercial" elements.

Many of Robinson's photos from the 1960s and 1970s make the game appear a dirty, muddy business – less sanitized. The sheer brownness of the pitches is shocking to viewers used to the brilliant greens of the modern playing surface. But he has also done his share of snapping the action and punting the image – that is how sports photographers earn their money.

The most significant change to the way photographers work has been a product of the narrow picture style often demanded by the mass-circulation papers. Television culture has forced football photography in the popular press in a certain direction – the single face/celebration/goal. Since the 1990s newspapers have given over more and more pages to football, which has meant a greater demand for football photography to help fill the space. However, as the story has to run seven days a week, tabloid coverage, in particular, tends to develop dramatic storylines and relies on a fairly limited cast of celebrity players. In photographic terms this has meant a trend towards using full-face shots of players. Another feature of the new aesthetic is to cut out the background so that the player is isolated on the page. Players themselves understand the convention and act accordingly; after scoring they will often run towards the photographers to celebrate and the celebration shot, especially if it features a celebrity player, is very much a money shot. The players know this image will appear on the following day's back pages. They also know which photographers work for the popular press, and it is to them that they play out their celebration rituals.

When looking through the Robinson collection it is surprising how close to the goal the photographer once was. Not only do Robinson's own images reflect this proximity to the action, but his wider views often feature the photo pack arranged either side of the uprights. Even the photographers themselves look different: today they wear fluorescent bibs, training shoes and weatherproof Gore-Tex jackets – technical clothing that mirrors the elevated status of football's 21st-century media workers. But in Robinson's photography the British snappers are old-school Fleet Street men in raincoats, sports jackets and National Health glasses. Television coverage bears this out: archive footage shows the goalposts flanked with photographers, whereas contemporary images show this area has been cleared – television demands unobstructed shots of the advertising hoarding, not a scrum of photographers. When we do catch sight of the photo pack they are pushed more to the corner areas, and they thus present modern football from a side-on view. This means that individual players can be more easily isolated within the viewfinder, unlike close-in shots where there is more likely to be a jumble of players and action.

Changes in technology are also having an impact on the work of football photographers. Most now use digital cameras and it is rare to shoot a match on film. Digital technology means huge savings in costs and images can be transmitted back to picture desks extremely quickly – photos from an important match will begin to appear on the wire almost from the kick-off. Speed, technology and the restriction of access could spell the end for Robinson's type of football photography. The levels of access once enjoyed by photographers are already a thing of the past. Clubs are far less willing to allow "outsiders" in, and issues such as image rights and editorial control have moved up the agenda. Indeed, will football even need stills photography in the future? It is possible to foresee a time where stills from matches are simply "grabbed" from television coverage and the football photographer will be redundant. This would also fit in with football's more governed approach to the media, and huge incomes could be derived from licensing off the rights to provided this service. The death of football photography may well be at hand: this makes the Robinson collection all the more poignant and historic. ***Fd***

previous page
Billy Bremner
Leeds United
c 1970

Croydon v Liverpool
Women's FA Cup Final, Millwall
Croydon win penalty
shoot-out 3-2
28 April 1996

2
9

3
11

Gola

Alan Ball
Everton v Liverpool
Goodison Park
12 December 1968

previous page
Manchester United
Old Trafford
c 1970

Salomon Olembe and Oliver Kahn
Cameroon v Germany
2002 World Cup
Shizuoka, Japan
11 June 2002

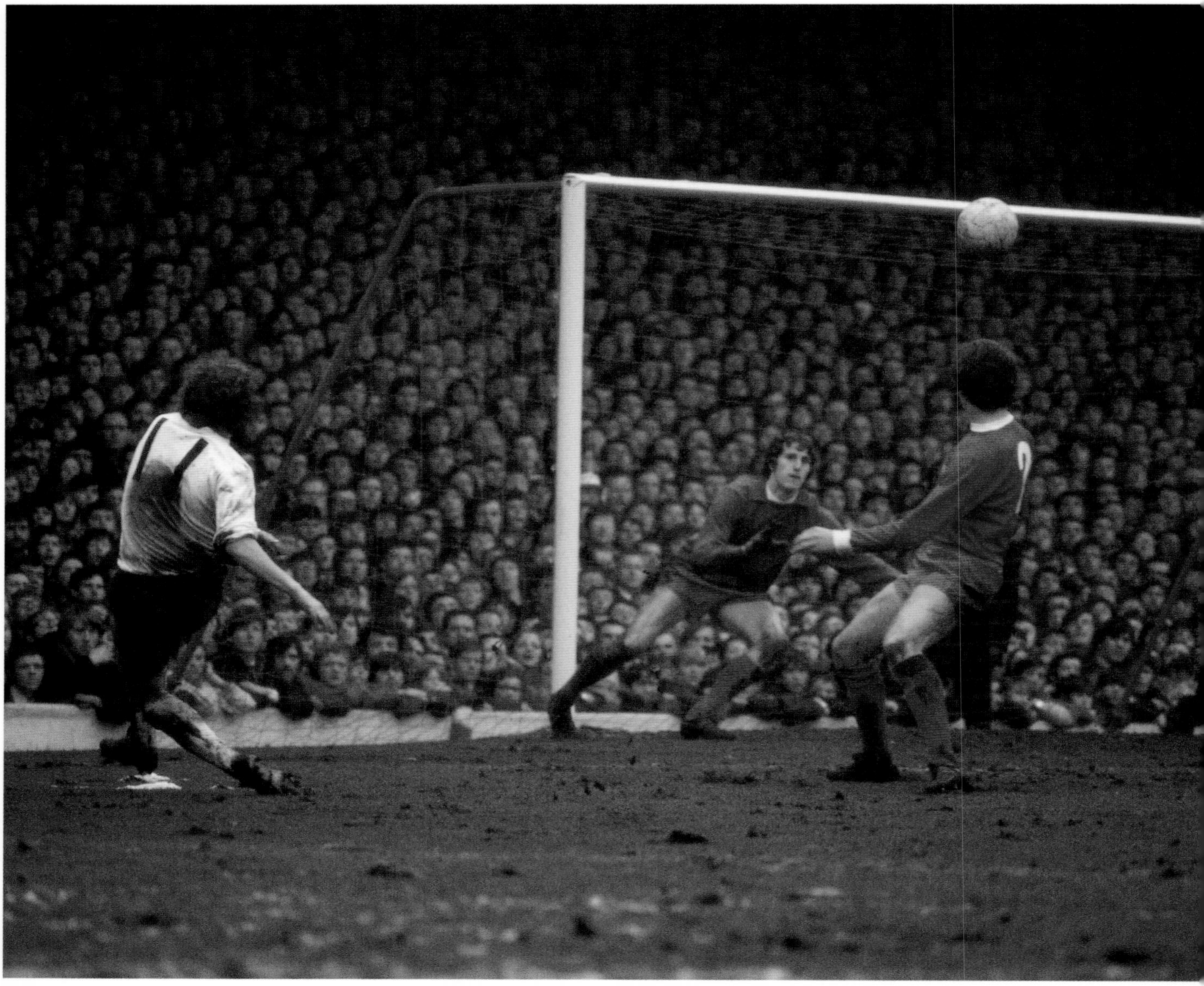

Liverpool v
Tottenham Hotspur
Anfield
18 December 1971

The City wall
(Left to right): Arthur Mann,
Alan Oakes, Colin Bell,
Mike Summerbee
Manchester United v
Manchester City
Old Trafford
c 1968

New Zealand v Kuwait
Players and police dodge flying beer cans
World Cup Qualifier
Auckland
10 October 1981

Old Trafford, Manchester
Juventus v Milan
Final of the Champions League
28 May 2003

Powerstock, Dorset
1999

The Baseball Ground,
Derby County
Brian Clough and team
July 1971

Leyton Orient
Brisbane Road
2000

EURO 2000 PLAY-OFF
ENGLAND 0
SCOTLAND 0
Coca-Cola
Nationwide
BURTON
UMBRO
AXA

Wembley Stadium
Euro 2000 qualification
play-off
Last England v Scotland
match at the old stadium
17 November 1999

Newcastle United v Liverpool
St James' Park
c 1970

Hackney Marshes, East London
December 1994

MASSACHUSETTS
STATE
POLICE
16

Italy v Spain
1994 World Cup
Boston, USA
9 July 1994

Bolton Wanderers v
Charlton Athletic
Reebok Stadium
FA Cup 6th Round
20 February 2000

Gordon Banks and
Jimmy Greaves
Stoke City v West Ham United
c 1971

makes the going easy
d the coming back)

AMS

Johan Cruyff
New York Cosmos
v Rest of the World
30 August 1978

previous page
Goalkeeper Steve D'Eath and Denis Law
Reading v Manchester United
Elm Park
Watney Cup
1 August 1970

Martin Dahlin, Sweden
1994 World Cup
Los Angeles, USA
16 July 1994

Birmingham City v Ipswich Town
St Andrews
17 September 1983

6
Brewers of th
idlar
DAV

Diego Maradona
Before extra time
Argentina v Italy
1990 World Cup Semi-Final
Naples, Italy
7 July 1990

Upton Park, West Ham United
School playground outside the stadium. Now a club car park
c 1970

adidas

2
6

Liverpool v Arsenal
1971 FA Cup Final
(Left to right) Chris Lawler, Emlyn Hughes and Ray Clemence after Pat Rice's equaliser for Arsenal
8 May 1971

Ireland v Spain
2002 World Cup
Before extra time
Suwon, South Korea
16 June 2002

1967 League Cup Final
Third Division Queens Park Rangers' 3-2 victory over First Division West Bromwich Albion
Wembley
4 March 1967

JVC

West Germany v Mexico
1986 World Cup
Monterrey, Mexico
21 June 1986

Denmark v Holland
Euro '92 Semi-Final
Ullevi Stadium,
Gothenburg, Sweden
22 June 1992

Johan Cruyff, Washington Diplomats
RFK Stadium,
Washington DC, USA
13 April 1980

AN
ARINO,
WHO?

Gerd Muller
Bayern Munich v Leeds United
European Cup Final
Paris, France
28 May 1975

previous page
Christian Chukwu, Captain of Nigeria
Lagos, Nigeria
March 1979

Neville Southall
Wales v San Marino
National Stadium, Cardiff
31 August 1996

Davor Suker
Croatia v Germany
Euro '96
Manchester, England
23 June 1996

Everton v
West Bromwich Albion
West Bromwich player in
crowd after victory in 1968
FA Cup Final
Wembley
18 May 1968

Pele's final game for Cosmos
New York Cosmos v NASL
Selection
Giants Stadium
Rutherford, New Jersey, USA
24 September 1980

Maradona's second goal
England v Argentina,
1986 World Cup
Azteca Stadium, Mexico City
22 June 1986

Goal by Alan Gilzean
Tottenham Hotspur v
Ipswich Town
White Hart Lane
c 1970

AWAY

AWAY

Much of Peter Robinson's career has been spent photographing football around the world. His connections with FIFA and a client list that featured many European sports magazines increasingly drew him away from British football towards the European scene. A childhood spent in the post-war gloom of the East Midlands followed by the early professional years travelling Britain photographing football at both ends of the spectrum – Northampton Town to Manchester City, Sunderland to Torquay United – made the world beyond seem limitless and rich in photographic possibilities. His first major overseas assignment was the 1970 World Cup Finals in Mexico. The opportunity arose through FIFA – but Robinson's original brief was to shoot the functions and committee meetings attended by representatives, and not the matches.

The physical and cultural barriers of the Cold War made visits to Eastern Europe akin to something out of a spy novel. Robinson recounts a trip to Czechoslovakia in 1975 with England manager Don Revie on a fact-finding mission. Visa problems had prevented other press men from entering the country and so the party was reduced to Revie, Robinson and a British Embassy official. They spent 12 hours watching the Czech national team play in Bratislava and checking facilities for the England team to use on their forthcoming visit. Robinson found it all surreal: the difficulties of entering the country, the hidden world of Communism, and the fact that, although he was sitting with Revie, the two men barely spoke throughout the trip – Robinson's presence was tolerated rather than welcomed.

A different time, a different world. Political regimes now consigned to history books, military dictators milking sports events for personal aggrandizement, countries that no longer exist – this was the world Robinson travelled, photographing football's outer colonies. The European scene held a particular fascination for Robinson, and during the 1980s he shifted the focus of his work to covering football on the continent. In particular his assignments for FIFA and the French football magazine *Onze* meant more and more time on the road. For Robinson this came as a relief as it allowed him to escape what he saw as the parochial obsessions of British football.

Robinson's disillusionment was born out of professional boredom, over-familiarity with domestic competitions and the increasing incidence of hooliganism that then blighted the domestic game. The endless round of motorway journeys and service stations had no appeal and he was, by his own admission, captivated by the glamour, exoticism even, of covering football beyond Britain. And why not? For Robinson, very much a privileged football follower, journeying into Britain's bleak post-industrial landscapes to cover matches also highlighted Britain's social dislocation. The rising levels of unemployment and material decay during the early 1980s helped fuel his desire to leave what he saw as a "sinking ship" and work somewhere warmer and friendlier, where the sun shone and the football was good.

He found what he was looking for in western Europe, above all in Italy, where the weather, the food, the architecture and the lifestyle revived his enthusiasm, and the football culture was more glamorous than the fundamentalist British game. Until the arrival of satellite television, British football fans received virtually no coverage of world football. The European Cup offered glimpses of different football cultures, but even that was switched off after Heysel. What Robinson was witnessing on his journeys was football on a far grander scale, magnificent stadiums, the best players from around the world and an alliance of artistry, science and tactical sophistication that produced a style of play far removed from the "kick and rush" approach that predominated in the British game. Ironically, until Heysel, English club sides had fared very well in European competitions. Liverpool, Nottingham Forest and Aston Villa had all won the European Cup during the late 1970s and early 1980s, and Robinson actively followed their campaigns, but these successes did not revolutionize tactics, training and team preparation in Britain. Perhaps this is what Robinson was witnessing on his sojourns in Europe, club sides attempting to emulate the success of English teams and in so doing moving scientific, technical and cultural understandings of the game onto a new level.

So much has changed in British football since the early 1990s that the cultural and technical differences between the top European football leagues are now less apparent. The Primera Liga, the Bundesliga, Serie A and the Premiership all vie to be the world's best competitive club league. In Britain, Sky TV money has brought an influx of overseas star players who have introduced different tactical approaches, more scientific training methods and generally a more international flavour to the domestic game. Perhaps "away" now looks less exotic from the British perspective as so much has been imported into the game here – plus, multi-channel television has brought into the living room football from around the globe. In terms of football fans "going away" to watch football in different countries and continents, this too is a fundamentally different experience. Until recently the World Cup Finals were alternated between South America and Europe – the two power blocs of world football – and few fans were expected to journey from outside their continent to attend the matches. As Japan/Korea 2002 demonstrated, "going away" on a trans-global trek to follow your team is now quite normal; a more developed travel/tourism culture and the availability of quick and affordable international flights have shrunk the world as far as the football fan is concerned. ***Fd***

previous page
Andorra
League Football Division One
August 1997

Malta v East Germany
World Cup Qualifier
2 April 1977

6
8

Brazil v England
Rio de Janeiro
8 June 1977

Boeing 747 bound for Sapporo, Japan
June 2002

Near Arras, Northern France
May 1998

Cyprus v Spain
8 December 1979

Near Rotterdam, Holland
June 2000

Lagos, Nigeria
March 1980

Azteca Stadium, Mexico City
Brazil v Argentina,
Coca-Cola Cup
19 June 1983

Singapore
Asian Football Championship
China player sent off
16 December 1984

SEIKO
JVC
Canon
POWER
CAMEL
CAMEL

Guatemala
c 1985

following page
David Vanole
USA v Austria
1990 World Cup
Florence, Italy
19 June 1990

Near Orlando, Florida
June 1994

Delft, Holland
Workman's cabin
June 2000

The
play
house
TOPLESS GO GO
FREE
WOR D CUP TICKETS
GAMES ON BIG SCREEN TV

National Stadium, Tokyo
European Cup winners Aston Villa training before World Club Championship match v Peñarol
December 1982

Beijing, China
May 1985

Tokyo Subway
After Manchester United win Toyota Cup
November 1999

「妙典駅」が開業します
SHARP

Kenya, 1982

Africa Nations Cup
Opening ceremony
Tripoli, Libya
5 March 1982

معمر القذافي
الكتاب الاخضر
الديمقراطية
الاقتصادي
الاجتماعي
FOR ALL

Mexico City
c 1982

Budapest, Hungary
May 1995

Bulgaria v Mexico
1994 World Cup
East Rutherford,
New Jersey, USA
5 July 1994

JVC
SNICKERS

Opening ceremony
Euro 2000
Brussels, Belgium
10 June 2000

Sakuragicho, Yokohama, Japan
June 2002

Cameroon v Nigeria
Abidjan, Côte D'Ivoire
18 March 1983

following page
Romania v USA
1994 World Cup
Los Angeles, USA
26 June 1994

Central Madagascar
April 1987

POLITICS

making soccer

SEIKO SEIKO
Canon

The end of the game
European Cup Final
Liverpool v Juventus
Heysel Stadium,
Brussels, Belgium
29 May 1985

Opening ceremony to World Cup Finals in USA
June 1994

UEFA President Lennart Johansson
Geneva, Switzerland
June 1996

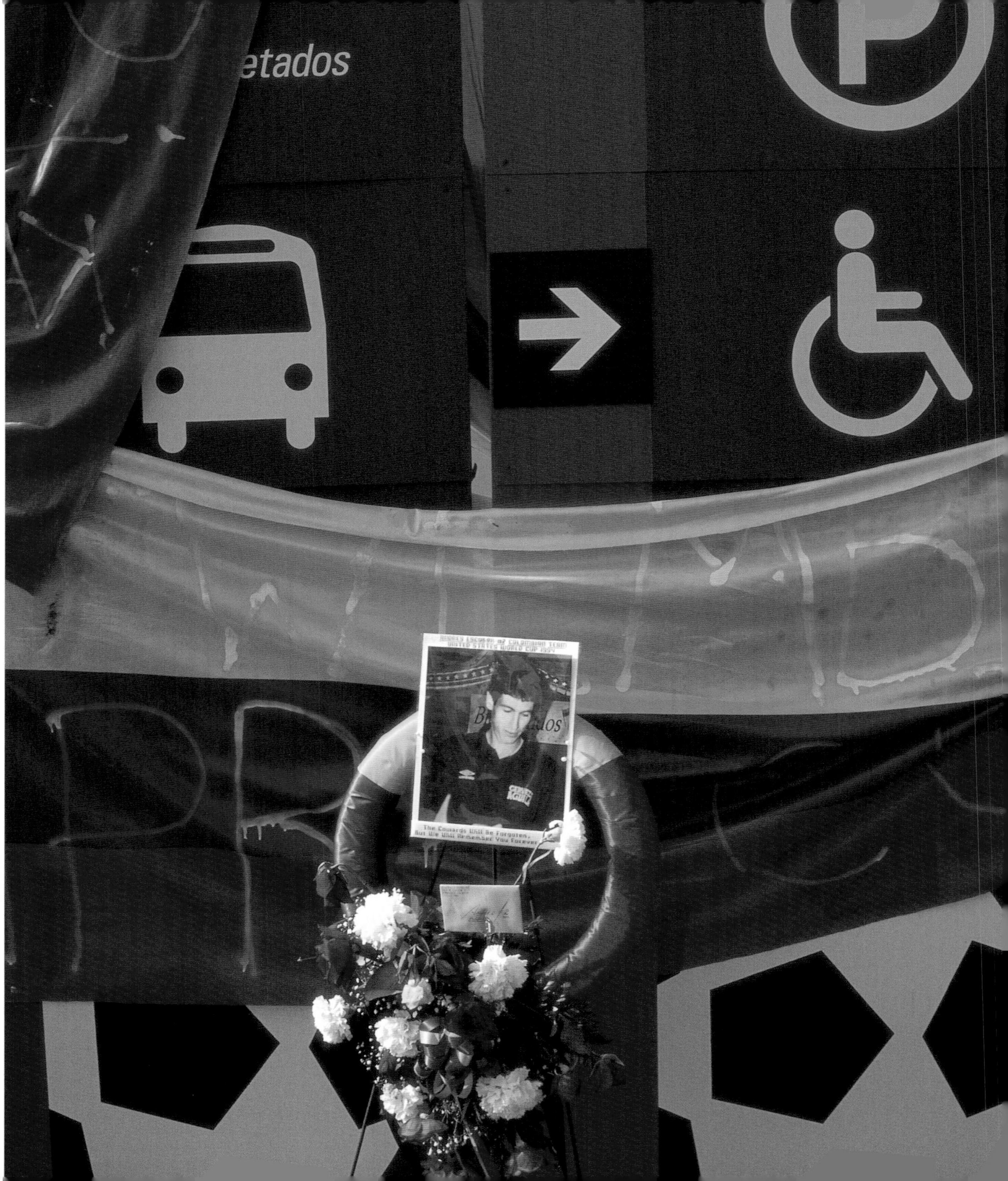
etados
ANDRES ESCOBAR #2 COLOMBIAN TEAM
UNITED STATES WORLD CUP 1994
The Cowards Will Be Forgoten,
But We Will Remember You Forever

31
Kunsthaus
Hegibachplatz
Konsum Verein Zürich
Liniennetz
Stadt
Tram
KILL
ARGENTINA
Nächste Verkaufsstelle:

Zurich, Switzerland
Graffito refers to 1986 Mexico World Cup, not 1982 Falklands War
2 July 1986

previous page
Memorial to Andrés Escobar
Los Angeles, USA
The day after Escobar was murdered in Medellin, Colombia, following his own goal against USA in the 1994 World Cup
3 July 1994

World Cup Draw in Las Vegas
US President Bill Clinton on a giant TV screen
19 December 1993

Diego Maradona
About to receive the World Cup from Mexican President Miguel de la Madrid
29 June 1986

Joao Havelange
In his last few days as
FIFA President
Paris, France
July 1998

UEFA President
Lennart Johansson
Athens, Greece
18 May 1994

AC Milan win European Cup
v Steaua Bucharest
Barcelona, Spain.
Centre is Silvio Berlusconi
24 May 1989

愛知県
西田
青山エン
青山
TOYOTA
CUP
村上 龍
TOYOTA
CUP
MR.GARY LINE
TOYOTA
CUP

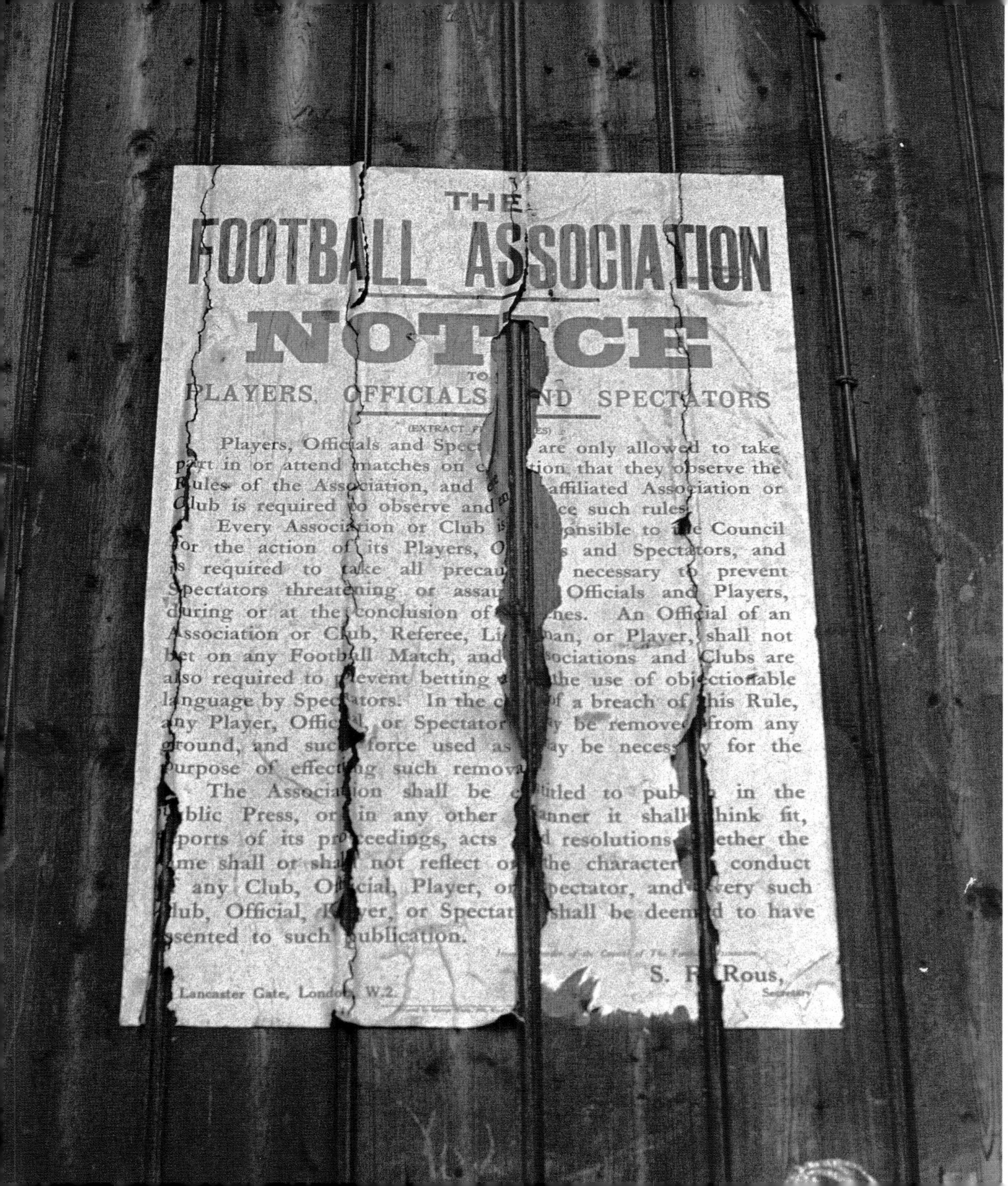
THE
FOOTBALL ASSOCIATION
NOTICE
TO
PLAYERS, OFFICIALS AND SPECTATORS
(EXTRACT
Players, Officials and Spect are only allowed to take
part in or attend matches on c tion that they observe the
Rules of the Association, and affiliated Association or
Club is required to observe and ce such rules.
Every Association or Club is ponsible to the Council
for the action of its Players, O s and Spectators, and
is required to take all precau necessary to prevent
Spectators threatening or assau Officials and Players,
during or at the conclusion of hes. An Official of an
Association or Club, Referee, Li man, or Player, shall not
bet on any Football Match, and sociations and Clubs are
also required to prevent betting the use of objectionable
language by Spectators. In the c of a breach of this Rule,
any Player, Offic l, or Spectator be removed from any
ground, and such force used as ay be neces y for the
purpose of effecting such remova
The Association shall be e titled to pub in the
blic Press, or in any other anner it shall hink fit,
ports of its proceedings, acts d resolutions ether the
me shall or shall not reflect o the character conduct
any Club, Official, Player, or pectator, and very such
lub, Official, ayer, or Spectat shall be deem d to have
ssented to such publication.
S. F Rous,
Lancaster Gate, London, W.2.

previous page
VIP passes for Toyota Cup Final
Tokyo, Japan
December 1998

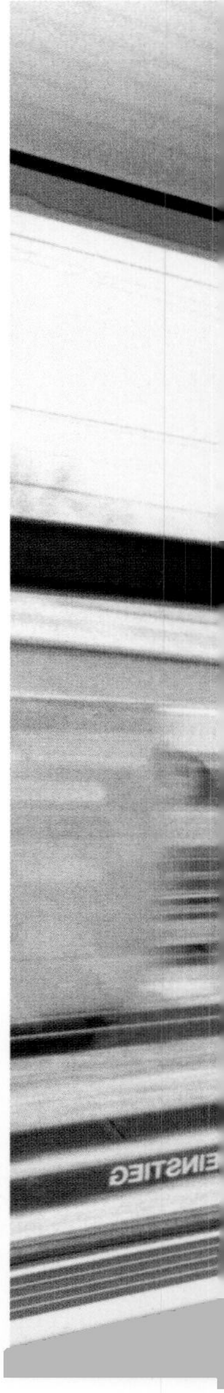

Workington Town FC
c 1967

Winners Yomiuri Verdy
Nabisco Cup Final, Japan
23 November 1992

UEFA President Lennart Johansson on TGV to Lille
1997

Ireland v Mexico
Orlando, USA
1994 World Cup
John Aldridge and Ireland
assistant coach Maurice Setters
24 June 1994

15
OUT
USA94

The Vatican
Pope John Paul II meets
FIFA officials
7 December 1989

Costa Rica v El Salvador
San José
16 July 1989

Argentina v West Germany
La Bombonera Stadium,
Buenos Aires
June 1977

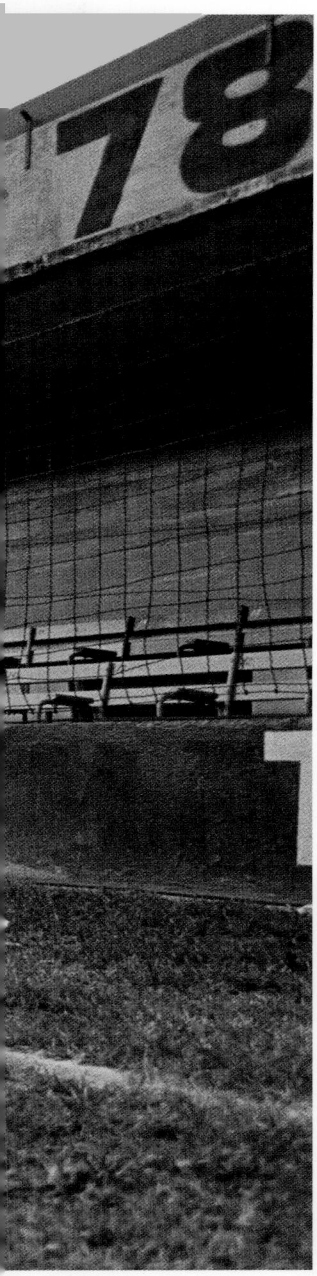

previous page
Diana Ross
Before Germany v Bolivia
Chicago, USA
1994 World Cup
17 June 1994

Angus MacKay, producer of *Sports Report*
BBC Broadcasting House
London, England
April 1968

1994 World Cup Final
VIP area
Los Angeles, USA
17 July 1994

FIFA
WORLD CUP
FIFA
SVT
BBC

Bernard Tapie
President of Olympique de Marseille
Marseille v AC Milan
European Cup Final
Munich, Germany
26 May 1993

Ken Bates in the car park
FA Cup Final, Wembley
Chelsea v Middlesbrough
17 May 1997

(from left to right) Franz Beckenbauer, Sir Stanley Rous, Johan Cruyff and Kazimierz Deyna
Victory banquet at Hilton Hotel following 1974 World Cup Final
Munich, West Germany

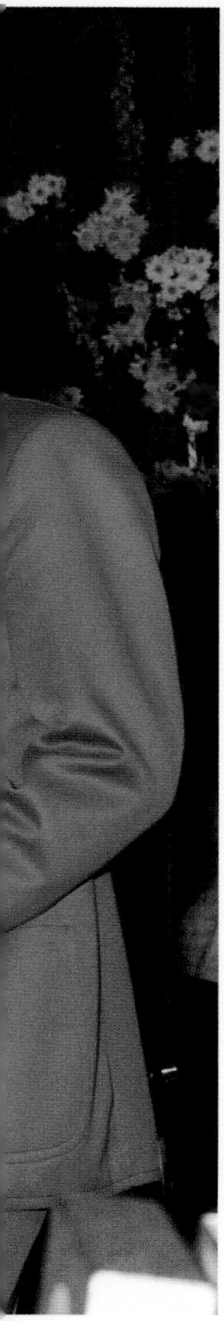

Red Star Belgrade with European Cup
Bari, Italy
29 May 1991

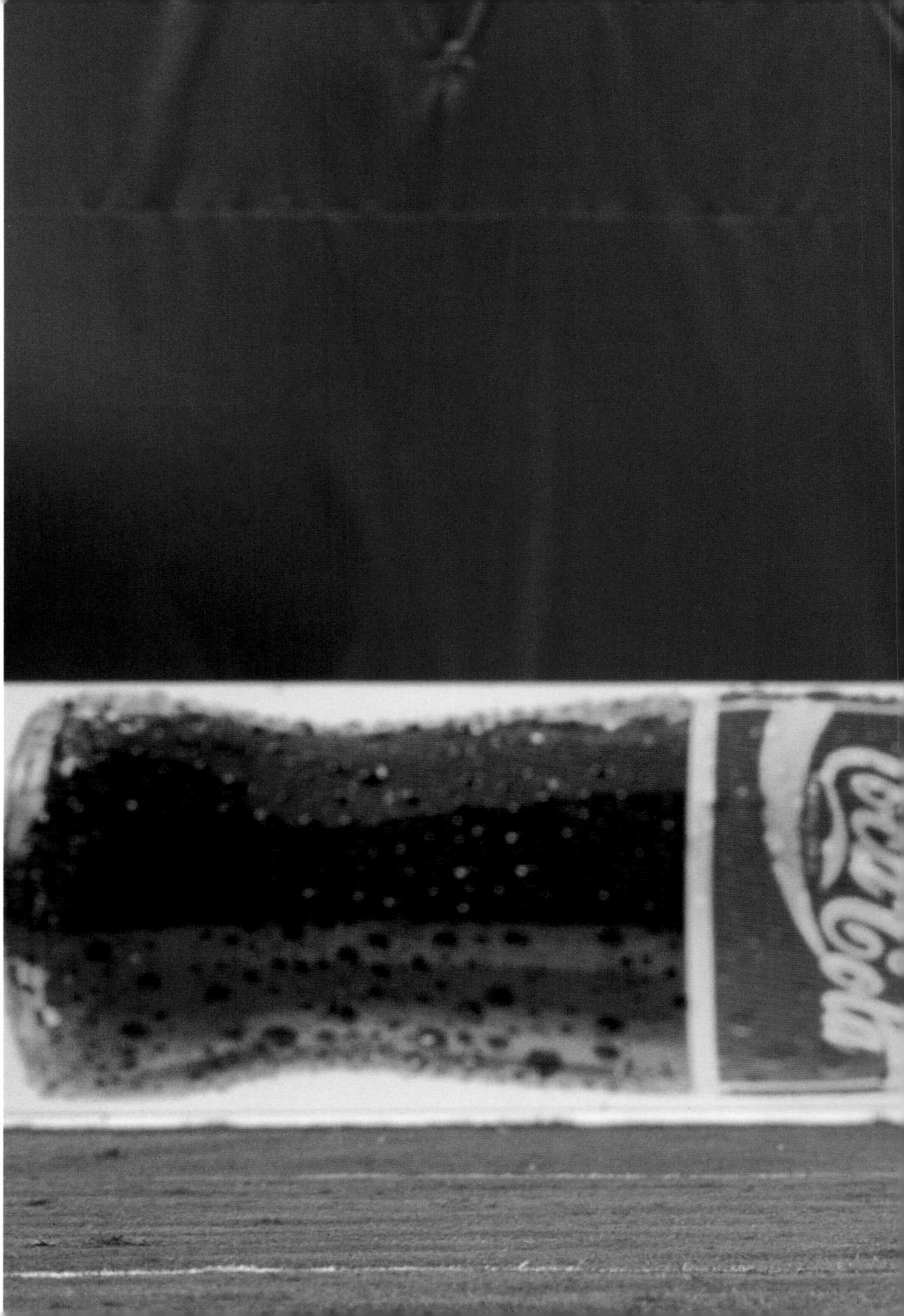

Emil Kostadinov
Germany v Bulgaria
1994 World Cup
Giants Stadium, New York, USA
10 July 1994

FAME

FAME

Football needs celebrity; the fame "thing" gives us other narratives to consider beyond the spectacle of the match. We now scrutinize a player's off-field life as much as we do his playing career – partners are photographed, lifestyles discussed and we constantly speculate about the material rewards on offer to top players. Football also creates fame and the game offers up some pretty improbable rags to riches stories; street kid to international superstar being the archetypal against-all-odds tale that, in one form or another, is enduringly popular. Footballing fame was always around, but it was more of a *Boys' Own* version of celebrity – play up and play the game, take the knocks and no bellyaching. Since the 1960s football has become part of a wider entertainment culture that includes pop music, fashion, television and the popular press. As a result, the idea of fame we construct around the game has changed, and it seems as if now we view football as an ongoing soap opera, a story without end with a familiar cast of heroes and villains.

Peter Robinson has photographed this phenomenon from the inside. His seminal 1968 images of George Best looking casual, cool, off-duty and relaxed in his Manchester boutique Edwardia – a cross between a super-rich mod and a French new-wave film star – place the photographer within the bubble of Best's life at that point in time. These images suggest a shift in understanding, a redefining of aspirations about the nature of sporting fame and the changing status of sporting icons – footballer as man-about-town celebrity, with all the benefits and pitfalls that come with this new status. Prior to the Best phenomenon – he was dubbed "the fifth Beatle" by the popular press – footballers had been viewed as essentially highly skilled workers, people who led extraordinary and privileged lives, but who were, nonetheless, working men. This status was captured brilliantly in John Fletcher's 1962 documentary *The Saturday Men* in which the camera followed a week in the lives of West Bromwich Albion players as they prepared for a match. What comes across is how ordinary their lives were: their profession gave them kudos within the community, but they were essentially "blue-collar" in terms of how they were viewed and how they viewed themselves.

Four years after *The Saturday Men*, England won the World Cup, the maximum wage had been abolished and players were beginning to enjoy greater freedom of movement as clubs were no longer able to retain their registrations. Perhaps this break-up of the old order which made players virtual chattels of their clubs altered our perceptions of them as performers. With higher wages and the increasing mobility of players between clubs, professional footballers became estranged from the world of work and community as understood and experienced by the majority of people. They were no longer artisan-craftsmen, but self-determining young professionals. Televised football added to the shift in perceptions as players became stars of the small screen, thus further changing our relationship with those who play the game professionally.

Robinson's career spans the time in which football has been increasingly positioned into the wider culture of celebrity. As a result professional footballers have become used to being viewed, objectified and gazed upon, like fashion models or royalty. Robinson's image of Keegan, Bowles, Channon and Hughes taken on an England tour of North America in 1976 hints at the changing status of professional footballers. They are dressed in tightly fitted casualwear, petal collars, bomber jackets, A-line trousers, perms and centre-parted hair – football as pop, footballers as pop stars. What is striking is their comfort, even confidence, in front of the camera. It would be hard to imagine players of the previous generation – the likes of Nat Lofthouse, Billy Steel or even Bobby Charlton – posing with such self-awareness. This process of objectification has now reached such a hysterical pitch that footballers are subject to ridiculous levels of prurient scrutiny in the popular press. The unrestricted access to the game's top teams and stars that Robinson once enjoyed would now be very difficult to achieve. He recounts a tale of being stranded in Naples after covering a match between Italy and Romania. Robinson had built up a friendship with the Italian national manager Enzo Bearzot who arranged for him to have a lift with the Roma and Italy forward Francesco Graziani. Today it would be almost inconceivable for a freelance photographer to find himself sitting in a Maserati with a top international footballer.

Fame and football once enjoyed a far less complex relationship. Players were well-known because they performed well in matches, scored important goals, played for successful teams and had long careers – that was about it. Some enjoyed renown beyond the sport, but they were few and far between. Football celebrity has now become part of the hype that surrounds the game. The role of the football star, the untouchable demi-god who enjoys limitless material wealth and global recognition, is to promote the game as fantasy. And not just the game itself. Since the days of Denis Compton's advertisements for Brylcreem, British footballers have endorsed products for financial reward. Commercial spin-offs are now ubiquitous and it is hard to enter a high street retail environment and not be bombarded with football imagery – advertising is awash with references to football and footballers. The game can seemingly be used to sell anything.

Robinson has photographed many world stars whose fame transcends the sport – Pele, Cruyff, Beckenbauer, Moore, Maradona, Ronaldo, Beckham. It would be fair to say that the football photographer helps to create the aura that surrounds these players, and contributes directly to the fame process through the production of iconic images. **Fd**

previous page
George Best
London
c 1967

Brazil Captain Cafu
2002 World Cup Final,
Yokohama, Japan
30 June 2002

S.W.A.T.
PATROL
LIEUTENANT

PATROL

previous page
Pele, the cup and the SWAT squad
New York Cosmos v
Seattle Sounders
US Soccer Bowl
Portland, Oregon
28 August 1977

Alan Ball with the First Division trophy
Goodison Park, Everton
April 1970

France win Euro 2000
Feyenoord Stadium,`
Rotterdam, Holland
2 July 2000

fifteenth
cup
CBF
BRASIL
CBF
BRASIL
CBF
CBF

Victory for Brazil
1994 World Cup Final
Los Angeles, USA
17 July 1994

Don Revie
At the Football Association offices in London on the day he was appointed England team manager
July 1974

Peter Shilton
Leicestershire
c 1972

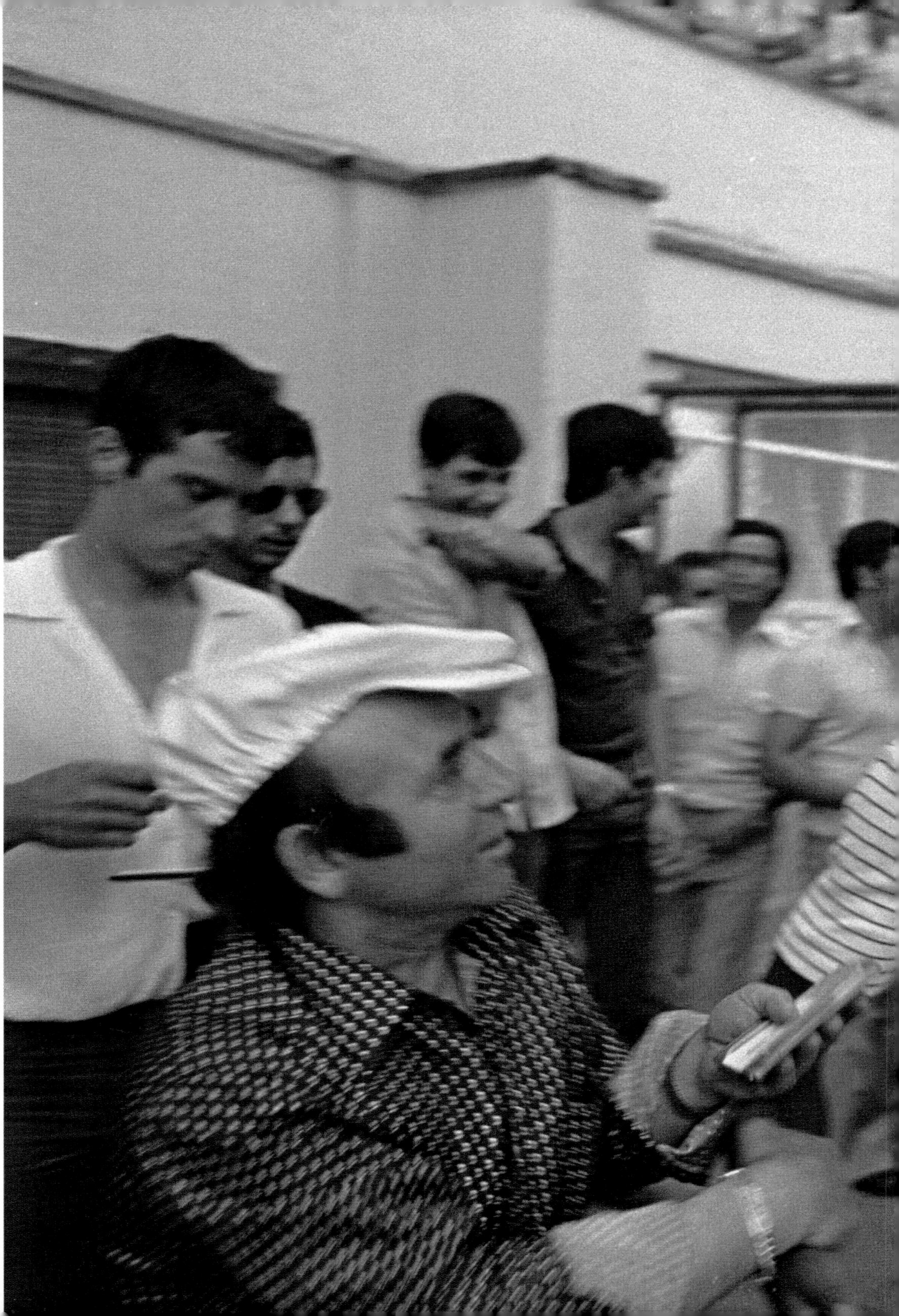

Laurie Cunningham
Real Madrid v Valencia
9 September 1979

Welcome to Azzuri's Tomb
YAHOO!
PHILIPS
FUJI XEROX
TOSHIBA
LOTTE HOTEL
FUJIFILM

Sudden death goal by Ahn Jung Hwan
South Korea v Italy
2002 World Cup
Daejeon
18 June 2002

Sven-Goran Eriksson's face on scoreboard
England v Brazil
2002 World Cup
Shizuoka, Japan
21 June 2002

England go out of the 2002 World Cup
England v Brazil
Shizuoka, Japan
21 June 2002

ulltime
AC3 Cambridge Utd 2-

DINERS
CLUB
BARCLAYCARD
makes shopping simpler
HERE
thes for men

George Best and Mike Summerbee
At their boutique
in Manchester
1967

previous page
"Keano"
Irish flag outside stadium
Lansdowne Road, Dublin,
Ireland

Teletext TV display
Cambridge United v
Crystal Palace
10 December 1999

Eric Cantona
Poster, Leeds
1996

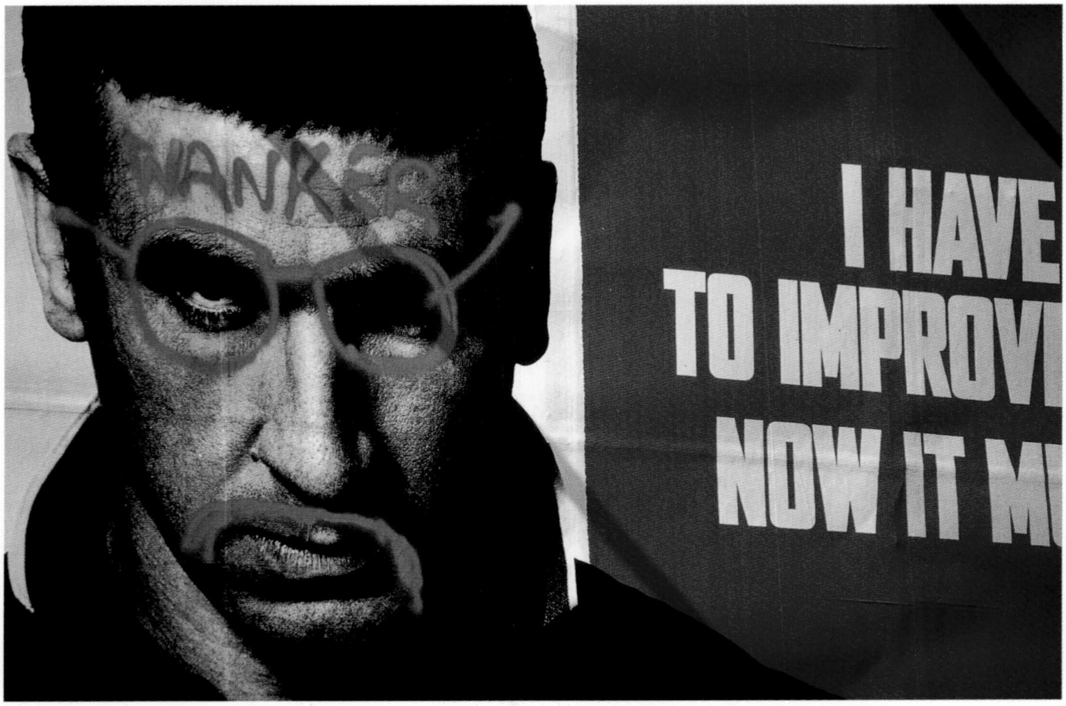

5 : 4
AL F. C.

Coca-Cola
Coca-Cola

West Germany before receiving World Cup medals
West Germany v Argentina
1990 World Cup Final
Olympic Stadium, Rome, Italy
8 July 1990

previous page
Valencia v Arsenal
Graham Rix fails to score from penalty
European Cup Winners Cup Final
Brussels, Belgium
14 May 1980

Cheerleaders
New York Cosmos v
Tampa Bay Rowdies
27 August 1978

Peter Shilton and Roy McFarland
England v Poland
World Cup Qualifier
Wembley
17 October 1973

Shrewsbury Town v
Newcastle United
18 September 1982

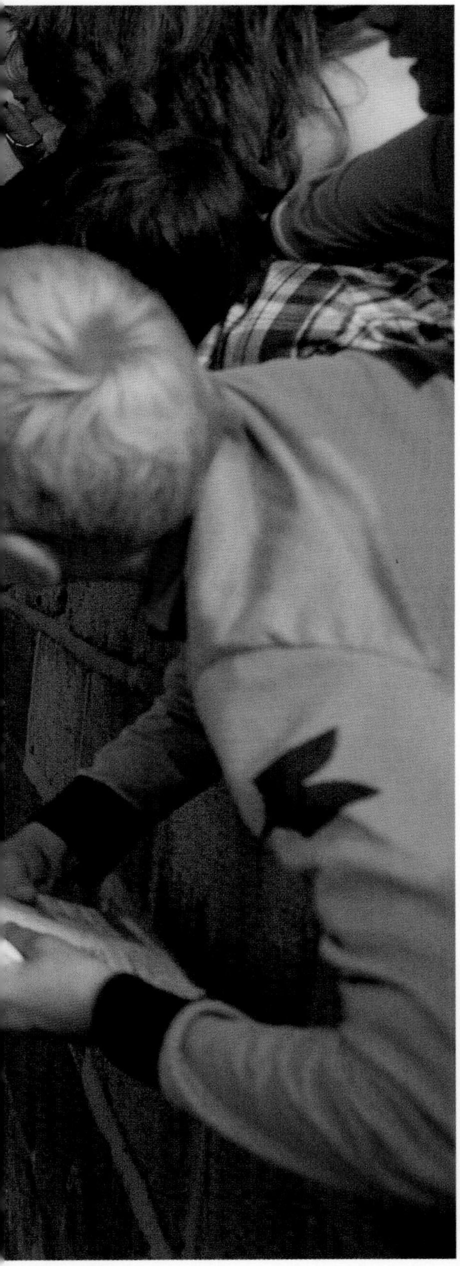

Youth international
Austria v England
European Under-18
Championship
Dusseldorf, West Germany
29 May 1981

Eric Cantona
Footballer of the Year Awards
London, England
May 1996

Waldemar Victorino scores the only goal
Nacional Uruguay v Nottingham Forest
Toyota Cup
Tokyo, Japan
11 February 1981

Ronaldo
Lazio v Internazionale
UEFA Cup Final
Paris, France
6 May 1998

Dennis Tueart, Mike Channon, Kevin Keegan Stan Bowles, Emlyn Hughes
England Team on tour
Los Angeles, USA
21 May 1976

81
106

FUJIFILM
SNICKERS
JVC TV & VIDEO
JVC
PHILIPS
MasterCard
OPEL

Brazil with silver medals
1998 World Cup Final
Paris, France
12 July 1998

previous page
Ruud Gullit
Benfica v AC Milan
European Cup Final
Vienna, Austria
23 May 1990

West Germany with the Cup as Holland collect runners-up medals
1974 World Cup Final
Olympic Stadium
Munich, West Germany
7 July 1974

PELÉ
10
NOT CROSS
DEPT.

Pele's debut for Cosmos against Dallas
Downing Stadium
Randalls Island, New York City, USA
18 June 1975

Nigeria v West Germany
World Under-17
Championship Final 1985
Beijing, China

Andreas Brehme
Argentina v West Germany
1990 World Cup Final
Olympic Stadium, Rome, Italy
8 July 1990

following page
Defeat for Italy and Franco Baresi
Italy v Brazil
1994 World Cup Final
Los Angeles, USA
17 July 1994

FIFA
WORLD CUP
107

FEDERAZIONE ITALIANA GIUOCO CALCIO
6

Germany team and flag
2002 World Cup Final
Yokohama Stadium, Japan
30 June 2002

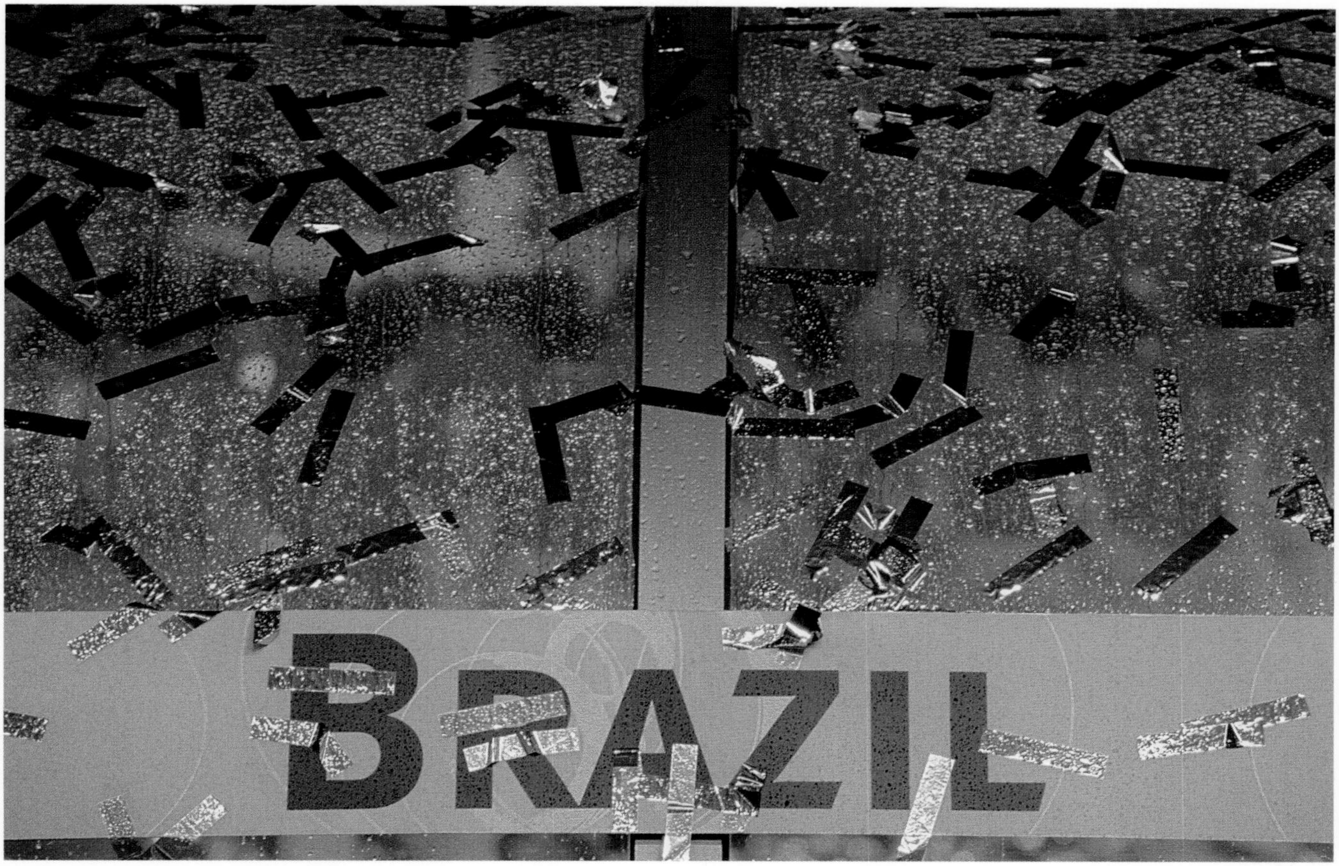

The end
2002 World Cup Final
Yokohama Stadium, Japan
30 June 2002

ES

CCCP
POLSKA

INDEX

AUTHOR'S ACKNOWLEDGEMENTS

To Michael Palin goes my undying gratitude for his wonderful foreword – a veritable mini-masterpiece. I am particularly indebted to Doug Cheeseman for his critical judgement and fresh and affectionate eye, not to mention his inexhaustible patience. A special thank you goes to our Referee/Commissioning Editor Mark Fletcher, who neatly side-stepped all my attempts at last minute changes in extra time. I am grateful to Kate John and the entire staff at Mitchell Beazley for their enthusiasm and dedication. Finally, a big hug for Will Hoon, who, apart from providing his insightful essays, had the original idea for *Football Days*. And a curtain call for the unheralded masses – the football fans. Their presence embraces many of the pictures in this book.

Alan Ball Snr
Division 3 Championship Cup
Preston, Lancashire, July 1971

PHOTOGRAPHIC CREDITS

The publisher would like to thank EMPICS Ltd. for their kind permission to reproduce the following photographs for use in this book: front jacket, front endpaper,p. 2, 5, 9, 10, 12, 13, 14, 15, 16–17, 19, 22, 23, 24, 25, 28–29, 30, 31, 32, 33, 34–35, 36, 37, 38–39, 40, 42, 44, 45, 46–47, 48, 49 (top and bottom), 50–51, 52, 53, 54, 55, 56–57, 59, 60–61, 62, 63, 64 (bottom), 69, 72–73, 76, 77, 78, 80, 81, 82–83, 85, 86–87, 89, 90, 91, 92, 93, 96–97, 99, 100, 101, 102–103, 104, 105, 106–107, 108, 109, 110–111, 112, 113, 114–115, 116, 117, 118–119, 120, 121, 122–123, 124, 125, 126–127, 128, 129, 130, 131, 132, 133, 134–135, 136–137, 138–139, 141, 142, 146, 147, 151, 152–153, 154–155, 158–159, 160, 161, 162, 163, 164, 165, 166–167, 168, 169, 170 174, 175, 178–179, 181, 182–183, 184, 185, 186, 187, 188–189, 190, 192, 193, 196, 197, 198–199, 201, 202–203, 204, 205, 206–207, 208, 209, 210–211, 213, 214–215, 216, 217, 218, 219, 220, 221, 222–223, 224, 225, 226–227, 228–229, 231, 232, 234, 235, 238, 239, 240–241, 242, 244, 245, 246, 247, 250, 251, 252, 253, 254–255, 258, 259, 260–261, 262–263, 265, 266–267, 268, 269, 270, 271, 272, 273, 274–275, 276, 277, 278, 279, 280, 281, 282–283, 284, 285, 286–287, 288, 289, 290–291, 292, 293, 294, 295, 296–297, 298–299, 302–303, 305, 306–307, 308, 309, 310–311, 316, 317, 318, 319, 320–321, 322, 323, 324–325, 326, 327, 328–329, 330, 331, 332–333, 334–335, 336, 337, 338–339, 340, 341, 342–343, 346–347, 350, 352 (left).

The publisher would like to thank Peter Robinson for his kind permission to reproduce the following photographs for use in this book: back jacket, back endpaper, p. 7, 11, 20–21, 26, 27, 41, 43, 64 (top), 65, 66–67, 68, 70–71, 74–75, 76, 79, 84, 88, 94–95, 96–97, 143, 144–145, 148, 150, 156, 157, 171, 172–173, 176–177, 191, 194–195, 200, 212, 233, 236–237, 243, 248–249, 256, 257, 301, 304, 312–313, 314, 315, 344, 345, 352 (right).

Sunderland
c 1969

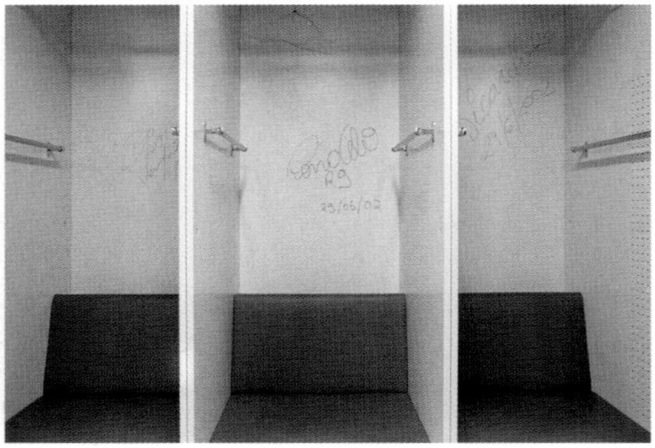

Yokahama Stadium
Brazilian locker room
29 June 2002